THE
MENTOR

TIM HENDRICKS

The true story of an hourly factory employee
who became financially independent.

Music City Publishing
NASHVILLE, TENNESSEE

Printed in the United States of America.

Published by:
Music City Publishing
P.O. Box 41696
Nashville, Tn. 37204-1696
www.musiccitypublishing.com

Designed by Lynette Sesler
Publisher's Cataloging in Publication Data
Hendricks, Tim
    The Mentor: The true story of an hourly factory employee who became
    financially independent. /Tim Hendricks

1. Success.   2. Free Enterprise.   3. Financial Security.
4. Character.   5. Wealth   I. Hendricks, Tim.   II. Title.

332.

Library of Congress Control Number: 2004116129

ISBN 1-933215-09-7

$16.99 U.S.   Paperback

Ralph & Betty Autry

This book is dedicated to

RALPH P. AUTRY

December 31, 1938 - September 12, 1998

Ralph and his wonderful wife Betty taught us to work hard, play hard, and sleep fast. They taught us how to make money, have fun, and make a difference in other peoples lives. They taught us that if you're not chasing your dreams, you're not really living, you're just existing.

"The type of person whom a child is taught to admire early in his life will largely determine the type of person the child will become."

—Tim Hendricks

What People are Saying

"If you only read one book this year to help you become more successful, this should be the one."
                                    Entrepreneur
"Reading '*The Mentor*' is a great way to become mentally and emotionally prepared for life."
                                    College Student age 21
"Most powerful book I've ever read on the personal changes required to become successful in wealth and spirit. Most books are written by the mentor (author) to the reader (student). This one gets into the mind of the student. We can follow his journey and understand the change in mindset required to succeed..."
                                    Dave Stevens
                        Commander, U.S. Navy (retired)

"I can't remember reading a more enjoyable, instructive and beneficial book in my life. It's very rare to find all those qualities in one book, but *The Mentor* is one of those rarities.
       I recommend it most highly!"   Pat Boone

From Pat Boone's personal letter to the author:
       "I read your book in one sitting last night. I was thoroughly enjoying and savoring your book, and have decided I want to go through it more slowly and read it again. It really is a wonderful account, and you tell it so well! I've done a lot of writing myself, and I really appreciate your style, your content, and your readability. It's pretty much the way I like to write, myself."
                                    Pat Boone
Christian, Entertainer, Producer, Entrepreneur

From: Bob Riley
        Governor, State of Alabama
"It is always delightful to hear inspirational and motivational stories. Thank you for taking the time to share '*The Mentor*'. Best wishes for your future endeavors."

From: Doug DeVos
        President, Alticor Inc.
"Tim, you should be proud of all that you've accomplished while building your business. Through Ralph Autry's mentoring and your ambition and drive, you have proven that anything is possible both personally and professionally. Congratulations on your achievements, and thanks for sharing your strategies for success."

"Both empowering and transformative, *The Mentor* shows how having consistent, one-to-one dialogue with somebody who's "been there, done that" can get you to your desired destination much more quickly than going it alone. ....Having a mentor is a key to reaching one's full potential...it can help a struggling protégé acheive phenomenal success...*The Mentor* is both a tribute and a guide, chockfull of little wisdoms that collectively add up to great advice for anyone who wants to live more abundantly."

Quoted from review by:
        Graciela Sholander
        Independent Professional Book Reviewers
        See entire review at: www.bookreviewers.org

"Anyone who has come to a dead-end, of whatever kind, will find inspiration in these pages. Tim Hendricks writes with an engaging "regular guy" outlook and sense of humor, but his book is a serious, valid road map from mediocrity to the winner's circle.

Tim's mentor, Ralph Autry, was a titan of a businessman, yet he knew that "a man's life consisteth not in the abundance of the things which he possesseth." His mentorship not only opened Tim's eyes to a way out of his financial dead-end, it also strengthened his commitment to "life, and life more abundant" through Jesus Christ.

This is a powerful book. Read it over and over again; give it to those you love."

Don Bassett
Chairman/CEO
Biblical Resource Center & Museum, Collierville TN

"Delightful reading! An exciting, stimulating presentation of how one can overcome dificulties and become successful in life.

The Mentor is an exceptionally and amazingly well-written book by a first-time author, who admirably succeeds in motivating and inspiring his readers toward personal success. Hendricks does more than just help us learn how to acheive financial success. In a most interesting fashion, he leads us to recognize and apply principles, guidelines, and morals that will pilot us to success in life itself."

Anita Kerr
Business Owner/Graphic Arts
Woodbridge, VA

"Terrific job! One of the best books on mentoring that I have read." Dennis Delisle
Entrepreneur/Author

Ralph meeting George H.W. Bush, Sr.
while he was the President of the United States.
Ralph's friend Brian in the background.

PREFACE

This book contains many of the lessons I learned from my mentor, Ralph Autry, during my quest for financial independence.

It is not presented as an all-inclusive handbook on Mentorship, nor is it presented as a 'how-to book' on achieving financial independence. The book is not about me, since I have achieved very few of the goals that I set for myself. It is very simply a summary of some of the lessons passed on to me that helped me to change my thinking so that I could break free from corporate slavery and economic bondage.

Also, please don't get the idea that Ralph was some kind of supernatural mystical guru, or even a perfect man. He was neither. He was an imperfect man with perfect intent. I was searching for answers and he was willing to serve as my mentor, my coach, and my guide, as he had served many others before me.

Since I could not find a definition for the term *'financial independence'* in the dictionary, let me give you my definition. I define *financial independence* as having enough money coming in to be able to maintain your current lifestyle without having to work at a job, career, or profession. Therefore, you are free to spend your time as you choose.

If you are searching for a better life, I am confident that these lessons will benefit you to the extent that you apply them to your life. Please don't just read the lessons, apply them to your life. I wish you much success as you begin your own quest.

Tim Hendricks

AUTHOR DISCLAIMERS

This book is based on my personal notes and on my memory, which are both fallible. If you know for a fact that Ralph didn't use the exact words that I have written, or if something was said at a different time or place than I have written, I apologize. This is as accurate as I can be with the notes and the memory that I have.

I would also assume that everything that Ralph knew, except for personal experience, he learned from someone else. He may have learned what he taught me from one of his mentors, or a book, or an audio recording, or whatever, I don't really know. So if you are the originator of a phrase, a concept, or an idea that he passed on to me, I apologize for not giving you the credit. What I have written, I learned or heard from Ralph. I also have never tried to verify any of the stories Ralph told me. Whether they were true or not was irrelevant to me. He used them to make a point, which they did, and that was what counted.

While I'm at it, let me apologize for any poor English you

might find. I write as I talk and I had the book printed just as I wrote it, so only a few corrections have been made other than the corrections made by the software program.

In my first year of college I had to withdraw from Freshman English class. I could read and comprehend just fine, but I didn't know a noun from a prepositional phrase. (Still don't.) So, to avoid failing and having an 'F' on my permanent record, I 'Withdrew Failing'.

Also, since I am not a doctor or a certified financial planner I would recommend that you see your doctor or your financial planner before implementing any suggestions from this book about health or finances into your life.

CONTENTS

Chapter 9

Chapter 10

Chapter 11

Chapter 12

Chapter 22

Chapter 23

The character of Ralph Autry.

Chapter 24

It happened just like Ralph said it would.

Endnote

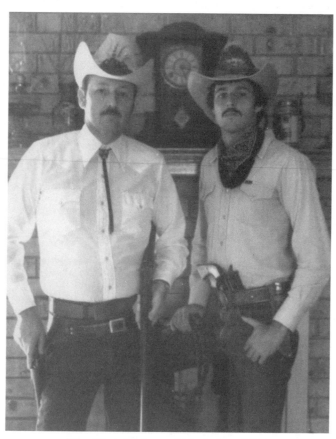

Tim Hendricks and his father, 1987

Tim and artist Dalhart Windberg, 1986

THE
MENTOR

The true story of an hourly factory employee
who became financially independent.

THE MENTOR
BY TIM HENDRICKS

As we stepped off the plane I saw the sharp young couple waiting patiently holding a placard with our last name on it. We smiled and introduced ourselves to them and chatted about the weather and our trip as they carried our luggage to the limo they had waiting for us. As we settled in for the ride to the location where we were scheduled to speak to an auditorium full of people, I noticed the couple sitting across from us beaming from ear to ear like they had just met a sports hero or a movie star. I smiled as I looked back at my wife and myself, and tried to see us through their eyes.

My beautiful wife of fifteen years was wearing her full-length, black mink coat with fox collar. The next thing that caught your eye, were the diamond earrings dangling from her ears. As the limo was already warm, she opened her coat to reveal a beautiful necklace. The dress she wore was a designer fashion statement. Our purchase had probably paid the dress designers home mortgage for several months. Her shoes were also very expensive and glittered in the limo lights. The emblem on the front of her purse told every female around who had designed the handbag. I personally wouldn't know a big name designer model from a blue light special, but the ladies seemed to know the difference. The ten carat amethyst solitaire on my wife's left forefinger looked great along with the diamond wedding band on her ring finger. Her right hand was nearly covered with waterfalls and clusters of diamonds. The diamond tennis bracelet and her Rolex watch could be exchanged for a small car if we ever got into a bind.

I had on a full-length black leather trench coat, Bruno Magli hand made Italian leather shoes, and a custom tailored suit with hand picked Gianni Versace fabric. My watch was German made, and the gold bracelet on my other wrist was worth more than my gross income for two months on my last job. The young man finally got uncomfortable with the silence and said, "So, I hear that you use to be a factory worker?"

"That's right." I said. "By the time I was in my late thirties I had been employed in over thirty jobs, and was working in a factory for ten dollars and eighty-two cents an hour. I dropped out of college after two years with no degree, and had no business experience, and that was the best paying job I could find."

As he glanced back and forth from my wife to me he had that puzzled look on his face and I knew the question that was coming next. I'd heard many versions of it many times before. He finally asked, "So how does an hourly factory worker in his late thirties, with no college degree and no previous business experience become financially independent in his early forties?"

I smiled and looked out the window at the countryside rolling by and said, "I found a Mentor..."

Author and his wife, Anna, 2001

～ · CHAPTER · ～

ONE

I see it on the television, in the newspapers, and everywhere I look. The economy is a disaster. More jobs are leaving the country every day. Technology is replacing more and more people every day, which means that more people are fighting over fewer and fewer jobs that are left.

Many of us are being lost between the 'cracks' of life. We need help, but we have too many assets for any agency to help us. We are forced to take jobs that have no benefits, no chance for promotion, and that barely provide us enough to survive on.

All of our lives we've been trained to become good employees. But, no one has ever bothered to teach us how to become successful entrepreneurs, the master of our own fate, the leader of our community, the CEO of our own financial empire.

From the time I left home at the age of eighteen I had been in survival mode. Living in people's basement apartments or cheap, run-down duplexes, sometimes getting to the point of having literally no food in the place and less than five dollars to my name, to get me by until my next paycheck on Friday. I considered myself to be a basically good person, but there had been times when I had to show a violent attitude just to survive. If you have ever lived in a slum neighborhood you know what I'm talking about.

I got married at the age of twenty-nine, so now we had two incomes and a little bit nicer apartment, but we were still living week to week.

I wondered if I was the only one that was unhappy with my life's situation. After talking with lots of people that seemed to be satisfied, I realized that they were not happy, or even satisfied, they had simply given up all hope of a better future.

I was not happy, but I had not given up. As a matter of fact, I was getting downright angry. Life was beating me down and I didn't know what to do about it. Everywhere I turned I was taken advantage of and no matter how hard I worked there was never anything left for me.

I looked across the table, piled high with bills, at my wife and said, "I just don't understand. I studied hard in school, I didn't excel but I passed. I got a job at a good company, I work hard, I'm dependable, rarely ever miss a day of work, I stay late, and work weekends when they ask."

"I do anything they tell me to do. You work eighty hours a week as a hairdresser, and we still can't make enough money to pay the bills on an apartment, a twelve year old truck and a ten year old car. By the time we cover the electric bill, water, gas, insurance, food, basic consumables, gasoline, a small church donation, the credit card minimums, and the other necessities, there is nothing left. I've figured out that the government gets over 50% of our earned income in direct and indirect taxes. About

30% off the top in income taxes, another 15.2% in social security taxes."

Years ago when they started taking social security taxes out of my paycheck I decided to check into it to see what it was all about. I came to the conclusion that the Social Security Act, as it was explained to people, sounded like one of the best acts the United States Government had ever undertaken, and yet it created devastating results in peoples lives in the end. When I questioned the age of 65 as the age that people were supposed to 'retire', I came across a statement by Professor Douglas Brown of Princeton, who was on the committee that drew up the bill, who said that someone suggested it, and no other suggestions were offered. He said, "The retirement age of 65 was set in 1881 by Chancellor Otto von Bismarck of Germany when he established the first known social security program. His actuaries assured him that few Germans lived beyond that age. It would, therefore, look effective and be relatively inexpensive." At the time that the Social Security Act was passed the average life span was about forty years. Today it is in the upper seventies. So, basically the government never planned on paying any of the funds collected back to the people who had paid into it all their lives. That's why there is no Social Security 'Fund', or 'lock box'. They collected all the money and had a great time spending it on other projects. They also did not include any inflation factors in the program. When they told the young people of that day and time that when they retired they would receive a certain amount of money per month when they retired, they didn't tell them that forty years later that amount of money would only buy about ten or fifteen percent of what it would buy back then. So people worked forty years expecting to retire wealthy, only to find out that their social security check would barely buy the groceries. So millions of people have worked their whole lives depending on the government to take care of them in their old age, only to find out that it was all an illusion, one of the biggest hoaxes ever played on people.

I rambled on, "They tell us that the company 'matches' our contribution, but that is just 7.6% they have to pay the government that they could be paying us instead. So it still comes out of our pocket."

"Then there is about thirty-six cents per gallon of federal taxes on every gallon of gasoline, 9.25% sales tax on everything else we have to buy, property taxes, and it just goes on and on. I don't know any way to legally get around paying taxes, because the KGB, I mean the I.R.S. publishes stories in the media regularly about arresting people for evading taxes. People who were sick of paying exorbitant taxes founded this country. They had a 'Boston Tea Party' and dumped all the tea into the bay to protest the outrageous 5% tax that England had levied on the colonies on the imported tea. The American Revolution started because of a 5% tax on tea alone, and that war broke this country free from control of another country so that people in the United States of America would not have to pay taxes. Now here we are paying over 50% of every dollar we earn to the government, and nobody even questions it."

"I just don't understand. I've read virtually every self-help book that has ever been printed about motivation, attitude, leadership, people skills, debt reduction, and financial strategies. After all these years of being the most highly motivated person in the building, trying to keep a positive attitude, trying to develop people skills and leadership skills, they still pay me ten dollars and eighty-two cents an hour. Having a positive attitude is great, but obviously that isn't the key to financial success. Leadership skills, people skills, and time management must not be the key to financial success either. I've taken the advice of radio and television guru's on how to get out of debt and start saving. Their advice helped eliminate some debt, but what they don't seem to take into account is that you will never be able to really get ahead by cutting up your credit cards and saving money, because the deck is stacked against you. I read an article the other day about 'product planned obsolescence'. They actually make parts for automobiles, appliances, electronic devices, and other things that have been designed to break down in a specified period of time, so that you will have to spend a fortune getting that one part fixed, or else buy another unit, which is what they want you to do. That is why they design them that way. So, about the time something is paid for, it breaks down and you have to replace it."

"Even when we do start saving ten percent of our income like the expert financial planners teach, by the time we have five hundred or a thousand dollars saved, the clothes washer goes out, and wipes out the savings. The next time it is the clothes dryer, then the transmission on the car, then the refrigerator, then the truck has to have new tires. About every six months there is a major expense that wipes out the savings. Medical bills, dental bills, central heat and air unit, and for people with kids there are new clothes, school bills, and recreational activities. Then there is Christmas, birthdays, weddings, graduations, holidays, and anniversaries to eat up your budget. I just don't believe that you can ever cut back, pinch pennies, or save enough to ever get ahead."

"Obviously it is not just our low income that is the problem, because we have friends that make $60,000, $80,000, and some over $100,000 a year, and they are always broke too. They live in big houses, drive nicer cars, wear nicer clothes, and eat better than we do, but they have to get up and go to work every day just like we do. Their houses and cars are financed and if they lose their income for a month or two they will be in trouble just like we would be. They are just broke at a higher level."

"Before we got married I even tried a dozen of the get rich quick ideas you see on infomercials and in magazine ads, but there just doesn't seem to be any way to make all those things work while holding down a full time job. You buy the stuff they are selling, which makes the people selling them rich, and the information sounds good, and is exciting, but there is never anyone there to help you make a practical application, or to teach you how to do what you read about. So you end up wasting your time and money."

I thought about a quote by Peter Lynch that said, "If you don't have someone in your life to teach you how to make money, who has made money, it is hard to learn how."

"I've read the stories of inventors and people who started businesses who got rich by inventing something or starting companies that change the world. People like Henry Ford, Ray Kroc, and Sam Walton, but what is the ordinary guy supposed to do?"

My wife was looking at me with that look that said, "I don't know what has gotten into you, but it's not my fault."

In the next few minutes of silence I thought to myself; whatever happened to the life I had before I got married. Life was exciting, adventurous, exhilarating. I used to go hiking in the woods, camping, fishing, hunting, exploring, and stay up late at night playing games with friends, doing stuff that was spontaneous, a little bit wild and reckless, but fun. Where had all the fun gone? Since I had been married there had been very little, if any, of those activities. It seemed as if my whole life consisted of going to work, coming home and doing chores around the house, and then falling into bed so that I could get up and do it again the next day, week, month, year....

On the surface I seemed to be responsible, and dutiful, a good employee and a regular attendee at church services, but on the inside I was dying of boredom from the dull and tedious routine. Since I had gotten married I had participated in very few activities or adventures that would get my blood pumping. I felt like a caged animal pacing back and forth dreaming of the day when I could get out and live free again. Sometimes I felt like life was trying to domesticate me, like a cow, so that all I did was eat, sleep, work, and get milked of all of my energy for someone else's benefit. Sometimes I felt like I was being slowly smothered, or strangled to death, and that created a deep down burning anger and bitterness within me. I didn't know what was causing those feelings or where the anger should be directed, so my wife was usually the one who caught the brunt of it when my frustration peaked and my temper flared. I didn't want to be a cow. I wanted to be a hard charging, dangerous rhinoceros, roaming the Serengeti plains. I wanted to be a hawk, floating on the breeze, wild and untamed. Free to ride the wind and risk the dangers of the world, to live with passion and adventure. Free to go exploring anywhere I wanted to go. I didn't want to be like the hamster at the pet shop, running on the wheel until it got exhausted, and crawled off to sleep, only to get up, eat, poop, and run again, over and over until it died.

I said, "I just don't understand. There has got to be a way to get out of the rat race and have a more comfortable, enjoyable life. What would be the purpose of living if you never did get to have a life? If all you ever get to do is to work at a job that you hate from sun up to sundown until you die, then they can just go ahead and shoot me now, and save me fifty years of agony. Maybe if we could just meet one of those rich people and find out how they did it, then maybe we could get ahead too."

My wife finally said, "Well staying up all night and worrying about it is not going to help. We need to get some sleep, we can talk about it later."

Ralph with George Foreman,
Heavyweight Boxing World Champion

Ralph with Dan Quayle, Vice-President of the U.S

・ CHAPTER ・

T W O

Not long after that conversation we decided to visit a different local church than the one we usually attended. As we drove to church services that Sunday morning I was still wondering why the rich get richer and the poor get poorer. I had reached the point in my life where I hated my job, hated the alarm clock, hated having a boss that told me what to do, when to do it, where to do it, who to do it with, and determined how much, (or how little) money I would get paid for doing it. I didn't like the quality of people I was forced to work with and I didn't like living like Pavlov's dog, with a bell that told me when it was time to eat, when it was time to relieve myself, and when I could go home. Since I didn't have to use my brain at work I spent time contemplating important things like: Why do they call them *apartments,* when they are all stuck together? Why do we park on a driveway and drive on a parkway? If you are driving at the speed of light and you turn on your headlights, will they shine? If a tree falls in the woods and nobody hears it, does it make any sound? How do you know? And how do they get that cream into the middle of those Twinkies anyway? I was definitely looking for a change.

The morning lesson was about how everything produces after its own kind. Pigs produce piglets; corn seed produces corn, etc. I was thinking to myself; rich people produce rich kids, poor people produce poor kids. Then I began to wonder if that concept would translate into the business world. If you could find out what 'seeds' a rich person had planted and plant the same 'seeds', then you would get the same harvest that they had gotten; wealth. Of course, you would need more than the seeds. You would need an experienced 'farmer' to tell you the best time of year to plant, how to prepare the soil, how to water, fertilize, weed, tell you the proper time to harvest, what equipment to use, and probably a lot of things I hadn't even thought of. So there again, just having the basic knowledge, or the seeds isn't enough. We're back to buying information from television commercials or magazine ads with no support. You need someone who has done what you want to do, and has done it successfully who is willing to take the time to teach you. And what successful person would ever have the time or the inclination to teach someone else everything they know about wealth. Where could you find someone like that?

As we were leaving, my wife said, "Over there is that couple I was telling you about who used to have an Excalibur; Ralph and Betty Autry. My dad and his dad knew each other."

I had told her before we got married that one of my dreams was to own an exotic automobile with pipes coming out the side of the engine compartment, called an Excalibur. At that time they cost about $65,000 dollars, almost three times my annual salary.

Observing the man and his wife from a distance, I asked,

"What does he do for a living?"

She said, "He's retired. He's had his own airplane and has a big house in an exclusive neighborhood in the Brentwood area. They go to Hawaii and Europe regularly."

By now I was staring. This couple had the lifestyle that I wanted and they were not anywhere near what is normally thought of as retirement age. Their two kids were teenagers. I wasn't aware of the principle that Ralph later taught me, but I knew they had what I wanted. I later heard Ralph teach, "Never take advice from someone unless they have the 'fruit on the tree' that you want." Meaning, unless they have done what you want to do, and have done it successfully.

I started asking around, and found out that his father was a gospel preacher, as was mine, and his parents were still alive, so he hadn't inherited any money. He had gone to college, served his country as a pilot in the Air Force, and had become a pharmacist. Then he had retired at the age of forty-two to become a full time husband and father.

I had learned by experience that every relationship in your life will move you closer to your dreams or further away from them. I remembered as a teenager, my mother telling me that she didn't like me hanging around with a certain group of kids because you tend to become like the people you associate with. I wondered if that would hold true, hanging around a millionaire and his wealthy friends?

If I could just get around them, find out what they had done, and maybe get some personal advice or counseling from him......

The phone rang twice and he answered, "Autry."

"Mr. Autry my name is Tim Hendricks. I understand that you retired when you were forty-two and it looks like you have a pretty good lifestyle. I'm in my thirties and I've been trying to find a way to get ahead all my life. I've had over thirty different jobs, tried a dozen different business ideas, and I'm currently working in a factory for ten dollars and eighty-two cents an hour. I was just wondering if there was any way that I could get together with you sometime, and maybe get some tips or some pointers from you that would help me get ahead?"

That turned out to be the first question I asked that would change my life.

He asked me a few questions about my current situation and why I wanted to change some things, and finally said, "Alright, if you are serious, you and your wife be at my house Friday night at eight o'clock and we'll talk."

I wondered why my wife needed to be there, and actually figured that she may not want to go. Besides that we already had plans for Friday evening since that was the one night I could stay out late. I normally didn't get home from work until after six. To get there by eight o'clock would be pushing me hard to get home from work, get cleaned up, have a bite to eat, and get to his house, which was about an hour away.

I said, "Well, that's not real convenient, uh..."

He came back, "Success is not built on convenience, it's built on inconvenience."

As I felt the hair stand up on the back of my neck I made a decision that would change my life. I decided that I would get the *facts* of how a wealthy person had become wealthy, instead of believing what I had *heard* or *read*. I said, "We'll be there at eight o'clock."

He gave me directions; I thanked him, hung up, and sat there staring at the phone. I had always believed that if it was God's will for you to succeed in a particular field, then everything would fall into place, come naturally, and be convenient and comfortable. Maybe it didn't work like that. I remember that after the fifth or sixth job I had quit, my motto became 'If the going gets tough, I'm out of here. This obviously is not what I was meant to do and I don't need any more of this crap.'

At the age of twenty-one I had decided that I liked western clothes; cowboy boots, big belt buckles, snap-up shirts, cowboy hats, and jeans. I hadn't owned anything but western wear for ten years and I wanted to make a good impression, so I got out my newest jeans, my dress up Lizard skin boots, my best silver and turquoise belt buckle, and my favorite John Wayne style shirt. I decided to leave the straw cowboy hat with the feather hatband behind, because I had worn it everyday for several years and many of those days had been hot and sweaty.

Friday night we jumped into the twelve-year-old pickup truck because it was the only vehicle that would start, and headed for the nice side of town. My wife had asked me before our marriage why I carried a loaded twelve-gauge pump shotgun in the back window of the truck. When you only earn seven or eight dollars an hour and you live alone, you don't live in the nicest part of town. I told her that I only weighed about one hundred and forty pounds and having Mr. Mossburg along helped equalize a lot of potentially bad situations. I didn't want to hurt anybody, but I was determined not to become a victim either. The truck got us there without any wheels coming off (which had happened before) and we entered what I considered to be a mansion. About seven thousand square feet on a hill, with two story white columns out front. The lots in the Oak Hill neighborhood started close to six figures and went way up from there. This was the neighborhood where the Governors Mansion was located. The state of Tennessee ranked Oak Hill as one of the two wealthiest neighborhoods in the state. He took us to his office, which contained more square feet than the last apartment I had lived in before we got married. As we settled into our seats I noticed the pictures on the wall of Ralph and Betty.

There were pictures of them with President George Bush Sr., the current president of the United States, Zig Ziglar, Dennis Waitley, Dick Vermeil, Pat Riley, Lou Holtz, Crystal Gayle, The Oak Ridge Boys, George Foreman, Ricky Skaggs, Jack Kemp, Newt Gingrich, Mike Ditka, Dave Thomas, Glenn Campbell, General Norman Schwarzkopf, Bart Starr, and other famous actors, entertainers, athletes and politicians. If I hadn't felt intimidated enough already, I was now.

As it turned out, they were very down to earth, friendly, and easy to talk with. They began by asking a lot of questions about our past and our current situation.

We explained that we had not been married very long. We got married when I was twenty-nine. Anna was older and had a sixteen-year-old son, and a twenty-year-old daughter. Because of her previous marriage, the age difference, and the kids, everyone we knew was against the marriage and had pretty much stopped having anything to do with us, because we went ahead and got married anyhow. We were always broke, no matter how many hours we worked. Both of her kids were still living at home, and they definitely did not want me there. Anna was a hairdresser with a shop on the square in the little town where we lived with a population of about seven hundred. I drove seventy-two miles one way to get to work at a manufacturing facility. We were both working seventy and eighty hours a week. I told him that I had talked with a lot of bankers and financial planners and the only advice they ever gave me was to 'cut back'. They said that the way to get ahead was to cut back and live in a less expensive house or apartment, cut back and drive a less expensive car or truck, cut back to less expensive vacations, cut back on your food budget, and on everything else. I told him that we were living in a place that cost less than fifteen percent of our income, driving twelve year old vehicles, hardly ever eating outside the house, and that we were not even taking vacations, so we didn't have any past due debts but we also were not getting anywhere.

Ralph said that it was always a good idea to live within your income, but cutting back wasn't the way to get ahead in life any more than slowing down in your car was the way to get to your destination faster. He said that his advice was to focus on increasing your income through a business of your own, learn to leverage your time through others, and learn to multiply your money through sound investments.

I went on to explain my frustration over positive thinking, time management, people skills, and all the other stuff I had read that had not changed my income by a dime.

He leaned back and looked up at the ceiling, "Imagine for a moment that you have read, and studied, and practiced until you have become the best race car driver in the world. We take you out to the racetrack and put you into a race with a guy off the street. Who do you think would win the race?"

"I would."

"Oh, one thing I forgot to mention," he said, "you will be driving a Volkswagen Beetle and the other guy will be driving a Ferrari. Who do you think will win?"

I had a mental picture of a Beetle going into the first curve as the Ferrari crossed the finish line. I said, "Obviously whoever is driving the better vehicle would win in a race like that."

He said, "That's right. It really does not matter how good the driver is. It does not matter how optimistic or positive you are, how good your people skills, leadership skills, time management skills, financial skills or anything else; if you are not in a vehicle that will take you where you want to go, you are not going to get there. A job is simply a financial vehicle. A profession is a different type vehicle, and a business is an entirely different type financial vehicle. What you have been trying to do is to apply your professional driving skills to winning the Indy 500 with a Volkswagen and it has obviously been very frustrating for you." He said that he wasn't knocking a Volkswagen, but that it was not a good vehicle for trying to win at Indy.

Ralph pointed out that the first step to achieving a better lifestyle was to identify exactly what you want. Then he asked what kind of lifestyle we wanted in the future.

I told him that all we wanted, was for neither one of us to have a boss, or a job, to get out of debt, and to be able to go where we wanted, when we wanted, with whom we wanted, and not have to ever worry about money.

He laughed and said, "Is that all?"

I said, "Yep, I don't care that much about 'stuff', I just want to be free like people I read about growing up; Huck Finn, Daniel Boone, Davy Crockett, and people like that who traveled around, got to hunt and fish and have all sorts of adventures, and just have fun. What I love more than anything is to go exploring. I've always felt that life should be a great adventure the way it was when we were kids when everything was new and exciting."

For a few minutes we discussed the implications of having that lifestyle and the kind of houses, cars, vacations, adventures and other things you could have if you achieved that much financial freedom.

He said, "Do you think that lifestyle is possible?"

I said, "Well, I haven't figured out how to do it yet. Since I've grown up and gone to work, its just the same old routine day after day, month after month. No fun, no excitement, sometimes I think I'm going to die of boredom, but after all, this is America, so it should be possible to do what you want to do."

Ralph said, "If you just wanted to make more money then a different job or a new profession might be the answer. Like getting a newer, faster automobile. But you are talking about having money coming in without having to get up and go to work. You'll need an entirely different type of vehicle because now you are talking about traveling overseas. No automobile in the world will take you across the ocean. No job in the world will give you that kind of lifestyle because when you stop working the money stops coming in. People who have that much freedom only have two things in common. Number one, they own their own business, and it has to be a business that can generate a residual, or permanent income, which eliminates most business opportunities. Number two, they have more than one source of income." He went on to explain that if you are an employee, or a self-employed person, all that you are doing is swapping hours for dollars. It matters not if you are the president of the company, the janitor, a self-employed welder, a doctor, or a CPA. You will never be free just doing that, because when you stop working they stop paying you. He said that if you earn a big income and live frugally, invest *wisely* over a forty year period, then you *might* be able to retire affluent at the age of sixty-five, assuming that the stock market didn't crash or correct just before you were ready to retire.

I said, "I don't make a big income, I don't know anything about investing, and I don't want to wait until I am sixty-five years old to retire and start enjoying life. As far as starting a business, I don't have the money to do that, and I don't have any knowledge, experience, or training in how to do that."

"That's about where I was at one time in my life. I was doing manual labor just like you."

I could feel my eyes squinting like Clint Eastwood in the movies. I said, "I don't see any similarity whatsoever between my factory job and a pharmacist."

"Pharmacists, doctors, lawyers, and dentists, are just highly paid manual labor jobs. It's manual labor unless you can get someone else to do the work. I earned more money as a pharmacist than you earn, but I was working eighty-four hours a week in the pharmacy to pay for our lifestyle. We had two children, I was teaching class at church and filling prescriptions for seven retirement homes on the side. No free time and financially just living month to month."

My mind was spinning, my eyes were still squinting, trying to find the link between a pharmacist swapping hours for dollars, in his mid thirties, and the millionaire sitting across from me who had retired from the pharmacy at the age of forty-two. The room was silent, almost as if he were waiting for the inevitable question. I finally asked the second question that would have a major impact on my life, "So how did you go from swapping hours for dollars, to being retired with a six figure residual income by the age of forty-two?"

He smiled and said, "I found a mentor." He went on to explain that a young pharmacy intern had approached him with a way to diversify and create a second source of income. Wanting to put his children into private school and unable to afford it, he decided to check into the idea. The young man had introduced him to a concept of creating distribution systems to move products from suppliers to consumers that required a minimal registration fee, no large investment, no previous business experience necessary, and flexible time requirements that would fit into an already busy schedule. He outlined the business idea on a legal pad as he talked. The intern also introduced him to a gentleman named Rick, who was very wealthy, who became one of Ralph's mentors. Rick had been a financially struggling schoolteacher until he had found a mentor himself, named Dexter, who had taught him how to become financially independent. Ralph later met Jerry who became another one of his key mentors. Jerry had been a textile plant manager before he started his own business and became wealthy.

Within five years Ralph's income from the new venture was triple his pharmacy income, so he had retired to be a full time husband to his wife and father for his children. He explained that he had shared the concept with a lot of other people and that many of them had replaced their job income with a residual type income through a business of their own.

That's what I had been looking for. He not only knew how to become wealthy, but he knew how to teach others to become wealthy, and was willing to teach others. At least he had been willing to teach others before he had retired.

So I asked the third question that would change the direction of my life. "Can you teach me how to do what you did?"

At first, he seemed to be hesitant, like he was contemplating jumping over a canyon on a motorcycle. Since he had just outlined the business concept, I understood that he would earn a royalty income from my business success, as a reward for teaching me the business, so I couldn't understand why he would hesitate at all. Looking back on that moment, years later, I understood his hesitancy. I was a basket case mentally, emotionally, socially, spiritually, and financially, and he knew that he would be taking on a long-term project with no guarantee that all his time and effort would ever pay off.

Finally he said, "Yes, I can teach you." Then he looked me straight in the eye and in a more serious tone he said, "IF you are willing to make some changes, IF you are willing to follow a proven pattern, and IF you are willing to get out of your comfort zone."

It was obvious that he was putting the responsibility for my success squarely in my lap. I stared back at him for a moment trying to comprehend what all was contained in those three conditions, but they seemed fairly straightforward. On the inside I was bouncing off the walls. Probably all that showed on the outside was a little bit of a glint in my eyes. I thought, if that was all there was to it, this would be a breeze. I'd be rich in no time. Now, years later, I understand how hard it is for an adult to change anything in their life. Even minor changes of habit are difficult, and major changes are excruciatingly painful. Following someone else's pattern is hard because most adults are very *do it my way* oriented. Getting me, and most other adults to get outside of their comfort zone is extremely difficult.

I told him, "I drove a steam train at Disney World, I've been a welder, carpenter, crane operator, radio station manager, forklift driver, backhoe operator, steel hanger, rod buster, concrete finisher, fast food store assistant manager, and a bunch of other things. If you can teach me, I can learn."

He said, "If you will do what I tell you to do, and follow my suggestions for five years, you will have a six figure income, and you will never have to work for another man for the rest of your life, if you choose not to."

I thought to myself, 'This is going to be a piece of cake'.

The next several years proved to be some of the hardest most frustrating years of my life. Changing the outward appearance so that I stopped looking like a factory worker and started looking like a businessperson was fairly simple. He had me read the book 'Dress For Success', and go buy clothes to make me look like a businessman. He taught me that people like to do business with people that look trustworthy.

He said that you need to look like other business people they deal with, for example their banker, attorney, CPA, stockbroker, etc. I couldn't afford to shop where professionals shopped, so I went and got myself some cheap black dress shoes, a black belt, a dark blue suit handed down to me from my father-in-law which had to be altered, some white shirts from the Goodwill Store, and my dad gave me a couple of ties with red in them. Everything else I owned was western wear, from boots, snap up shirts, big belt buckles, and wide leather belts. I thought I looked pretty sharp in my new 'business uniform'. Looking back at pictures from those days I looked more like a common laborer in a poorly fitting suit, than like a professional, but that outfit got me by until I could afford some nicer things.

Then I had my shoulder length hair cut short and neatly trimmed, so I could be a 'bidness man'. That's what they started calling me at work, (among other things not nearly as polite). My co-workers all thought I was crazy. They said, "Do you really think that hanging around with that rich guy is going to help you get rich?"

I said, "Well, actually, yes." They laughed at me and ridiculed me from that day on. I guess their mothers never told them how associations could affect you. They all still work at the factory or other menial labor jobs. (He who laughs last, does it on the beaches in Hawaii.)

I found out that most professionals are clean-shaven, but I couldn't part with the mustache I'd had for nine years until almost a year later, when I started seeing the real potential of owning a successful business. I also liked my long, Elvis-like sideburns *(thank you very much)*, so it took a while for them to go. The outward transformation was relatively easy. The inward transformation from employee mentality to business owner mentality, from poor self-image to healthy self-image, from very shy, introverted and easily intimidated, to confident self assured and totally unintimidatable, took me about two years. (I'm not sure *unintimidatable* is a word, but I think you get the point.)

Ralph said, "Those things you acquire with the most difficulty you will retain the longest and they will be of the most value to you."

I had always believed that you had to be incredibly wise to become financially independent. Ralph said, "You don't have to know all the answers to be wise. A wise man knows what questions to ask, and he knows to only ask those questions of people who are in a position to know the answers."

I won't describe in detail all the changes I went through, all the struggles and challenges I had to overcome, because that would fill several books. Besides, most of you live in the same world I live in and you are already familiar with the struggles and challenges of life. I'll begin each segment with a statement, question, or situation I had, and then relate to you, the knowledge and wisdom that my mentor passed on to me in the hopes that it will also help you. In truth, I learned a tremendous amount from both Ralph and Betty, but in this book I want to focus on things I learned from Ralph. The things that we learned from Betty would fill another book.

The only thing he asked in return for teaching me how to become financially independent, was that once I had gotten to that point, that I would share the knowledge that he had passed on to me with as many other people as possible. I've been doing that for years with individuals, but someone finally pointed out to me that I could help a lot more people if I would just write it all down. So this book was written as a tribute to him, and to fulfill that promise. My hope is that you will also be willing to share your knowledge and wisdom with others as you experience more and more success in your life.

I was instructed to be in contact with him on a regular basis by phone or voicemail. We got together in person at least every two weeks. It became obvious very quickly that he didn't need me; I needed him. So I determined that I would have to pursue him in order to learn from him. He didn't chase me down and try to teach me things that I wasn't ready for. He waited until I sought him out and asked questions, and then he gave me what I needed to know to succeed. I knew that he had the wisdom and knowledge that I needed to be able to accomplish what he had accomplished, so I determined that it would be worth whatever price I had to pay to get that knowledge and information. For me to be able to go to where he was accessible took a certain amount of time, a certain amount of money, and some dedicated effort. But, for me, the prize of total financial and personal freedom was worth the price. Ralph spent a lot of time with his family and doing things that he enjoyed doing, so I couldn't just get together with him and 'hang out', he didn't like sitting around doing nothing, so most of the time I had to get with him when he was going about his business in a time and place where I had access to him. So that he wouldn't mind me being around so much, I tried to be of as much service to him as I could. I did whatever I could to make his life easier, in exchange for him passing on a lifetime of experiences and wisdom to me. If I asked him to go out to eat, I paid.

(Sometimes when I asked to get together, he would suggest that we meet at a restaurant, and then he would pay, which was good, because I usually couldn't afford the places he suggested.) If we were going to a meeting, I always offered to carry his luggage, briefcase or materials, leaving him free to interact with the people, so that I could observe. If he needed something, I would offer to go and get it. Many people will read this paragraph and think; well I don't want to be somebody else's gopher! You may not have to. That is the price that I determined to pay. Just remember the prize, a six figure residual income.

I decided that it would be worth it. I also enjoyed the time I got to spend with my mentor, who became my best friend. It wasn't him who expected me to be of service to him, because he had a servant heart himself; it was me who willingly put myself in that position.

I also made it a habit to carry a notepad with me whenever I was with him to take notes on what he said. Sometimes I knew that what he said was very important, and sometimes I felt like what he had just said must have gone right over my head, because I didn't get the point, but I wrote it down anyway. It may have been weeks later, sometimes years later, as I reviewed my notes, that what he had said would finally hit home, because I was at a point in my life where I could comprehend and accept what he had been trying to teach me. To this day, I still take notes when I am around someone I want to learn from. There are lots of things I wrote down from what Ralph or others said that could not be put into this book, so I am putting some of them on my website that you can access at www.musiccitypublishing.com/timhendricks.htm

Though my mentor was retired from the corporate world, he still managed to find five or ten hours a week to keep his finger on the pulse of his business. So I started going to the places where I knew that he would be, any time that I could. Sometimes it would be getting together with some of his key people; sometimes he would be a guest speaker at a seminar or training session, or at a major convention. I told him one time, "For the next couple of years, every time you turn around you are going to bump into me, because I'm going to be right here by your hip pocket, looking over your shoulder, watching what you do and how you do it, listening and learning, until I can do what you do."

Over the years I noticed that a lot of people were attracted to Ralph and Betty and the other leaders and, like me, they wanted to be around them. However when they were with them the new people wanted to run their mouth about themselves, what they wanted to do, what they planned on doing, how great they were going to be, etc. I also noticed that the people who talked instead of listening didn't ever learn how to become successful. I figured that I could only learn something new if I was listening.

So most of the time I kept my mouth shut and tried to stay out of the way, but I was right there watching and learning. Several years later after I had retired from my factory job, we were both speaking at a seminar, and a man came walking up to introduce a new business partner to Ralph. Being in the same industry I had seen him around, but didn't know him personally.

His introduction went like this, "John, this is Ralph Autry, the man I've been telling you about, and this is Tim Hendricks, one of his business partners. Every time you see Ralph Autry you'll see Tim Hendricks right beside him."

I had to smile. I had recently retired from my job to run my own business while still in my thirties. We had just returned from our first weeklong trip to Hawaii, and we had just purchased the first brand new car we had ever been able to purchase, which cost more money than I had made in a year at my factory job.

My mom was right. You do tend to become like the people you hang around with.

A few weeks after Ralph and Betty agreed to work with us he told us that they were going to a convention for his business, which was to be held in San Destin, Florida. He said that we needed to be there because one convention would take about six months off of the time that it would take to become financially independent. The entire trip would cost us as much as we both brought home in a week, which we didn't have, but I decided that to reach financial freedom six months sooner, I couldn't afford to miss it. We had already decided that we would do whatever they told us to do as long as it was legal, moral, and ethical, which it always was, so we did whatever we had to do to scrape together the money to go.

On Thursday afternoon, before the convention began on Friday, they had a beach party for all of the leaders. I'm reasonably sure that we did not qualify to be there, but since it was Ralph's business he could invite anyone he chose to invite.

It was an eye opening experience for me. Here was a group of people who obviously loved life, loved having fun, and were very down to earth, even though some were very wealthy. Everyone had a great time without any artificial stimulants like alcohol, drugs, or wacky weed. I also noticed that there was no cursing, swearing, fighting, or hitting on other peoples spouses, which were all a normal part of the activities of the people I worked with in the factory.

We got the chance to meet and get to know some of Ralph and Betty's closest friends from around the country, Brian and Judy, Alan and Stephanie, and others. I decided that very weekend that these were the type people that I would like to spend my life with. People that I could respect, admire, and trust, and people that I would not mind being around my family. I also decided that if the wealthy could play at world-class locations like this, then I wanted to join them.

When I mentioned to Ralph that I would like to become wealthy so that I could live like this, he said, "Becoming wealthy takes time, effort, and commitment now, so that you can enjoy life *later*. Most people want to use all of their time trying to enjoy life right now. If you pay now, you'll play later; if you play now, you'll pay later. To get ahead and stay ahead in life you must have dreams that you are currently chasing as well as bigger dreams waiting in the wings. Success doesn't sneak up and grab anybody. The preparations have been in the making for years."

Toward the end of the beach party we were sitting at a picnic table watching the sunset and Ralph told me an interesting little story.

"One of my favorite stories is the one about a young boy playing on the beach early one morning after a storm. As he is playing he observes an old man slowly walking down the beach. Every few steps the old man stops, bends over, picks something up, wades out into the surf, and gently puts it down into the water. The young boy watches as the old man continues this routine several times. Finally the boy's curiosity gets the best of him, so he gets up and walks down the beach to where the old man is coming back out of the water.

The boy says, I hope you don't mind my asking, but, what are you doing?

The old man smiles and points up and down the beach and says, Well, because of last nights storm there are starfish that have washed up on the beach, and if someone doesn't help them get back into the water, they'll dry up and die. So I'm putting them back into the water.

The boy looks up the beach at all the sea creatures that had been washed up on the shore and says to the old man, I don't see any sense in that. There are hundreds of them on this beach alone, and there are beaches all over the world. There is no way that you can even get all of them on this beach back into the water before they die, so what difference does it make?

The old man's smile fades away as he looks down at the boy, then without saying a word he reaches down and picks up a starfish. Its outer surface already becoming dry and hard, but underneath, it is still soft and moist, hanging on desperately to its life. He walks out into the water and submerges the creature and watches as it is quickly revived and begins to move, as he releases it to make its way back out to sea. As he comes back out of the water he stops in front of the young man who is still watching intently, and says, I made a difference to that one."

Sitting there on the beach with the surf rolling in, it was easy to visualize that story. I could see myself as the young boy full of curiosity. I said, "That's an interesting story." I didn't say it out loud, but I was thinking to myself, 'So what if you do save one starfish out of millions that have been washed up on the shore, in the big scheme of things, what difference does it make?'

San Destin Resort was an incredible place. I decided that if this was how the wealthy lived, I needed to join them. The convention was a life changing experience that can't be described on paper. Imagine trying to describe a banana to someone who had never seen or tasted one. How would you describe the taste? It would be that difficult to describe our conventions. You would have to attend one yourself to understand the powerful impact that it could have on your life. If you ever get invited to attend a weekend convention I would highly recommend going. Just go in with an open mind and it just might change your life for the better.

Ralph & Betty with entertainer Barbara Mandrell

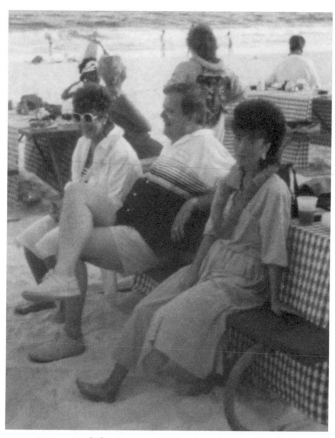

Betty, Ralph, Anna at San Destin Beach Party

⌐◦ · CHAPTER · ◦⌐

THREE

After reviewing the information pack that Ralph had sent me home with, and after checking the legality of the business with the state Attorney's general office, the Better Business Bureau, and the Federal Trade Commission, I had decided that I would be brain dead if I didn't pursue the opportunity. I was broke, Ralph was doing real well, and he was going to teach me the system that he had used to get that way, and actually help me to get started without me having to pay him.

I had also asked some of my family, friends, and co-workers what they thought of the business idea. That was brilliant on my part. Ask a factory worker what he thinks about a business with a six-figure income potential. I found out real quick that every one has an opinion on every subject, even if they have absolutely no knowledge of the subject. Some people even got hostile at just the mention of a business where you could create a second source of income. I didn't know where the hostility came from, but it couldn't have been my fault, all I did was ask a simple question. At any rate, none of those people helped me pay my bills and none of them had a better plan to get ahead than the one Ralph had explained, so I decided to stick with Ralph.

I had asked my mentor if I could get with him to learn more about how to get my business started. He gave me a time to be at his house. As I pulled in, he came out and said, "Hop into the Cadillac, I've got some things I need to do. We can talk as we ride."

I noticed that the Cadillac didn't ride like my old pick-up truck. The leather seats were nice; the ride was smooth and quiet. We went to the Lexus dealership. He said he was trying to decide what his next car would be. So as we sat in different models I would ask him about business and he would give me a short answer and then point out the quality of this car, the comfort of that one, the speed and quietness of a Lexus. I had realized that in order to get specific information from him, I had to clearly define for him what it was that I wanted, or needed. So I always began by asking questions. They may or may not have been the right questions to ask at that point in time, but he always seemed to be able to give me the right answers, even if I had not asked the right questions. So I would ask the best question I could come up with, and then shut up and listen. I had never been in a Lexus before and it was very different from the 1974 Jeep pick-up truck I drove.

In response to one question, he said, "The first thing that you need to realize is that we are in the people business. Some people think they are in the insurance business, or real estate, or accounting, or engineering, manufacturing, direct sales, network marketing, legal services, wholesale, or retail, but in reality they are all in the people business. They just have different business vehicles to take them where they want to go financially. Without people there would be no need for businesses to supply products and services. You can call them customers, clients, affiliates, partners, or whatever, but people are the key to making a business profitable. Becoming better at building relationships is not optional if you want to be successful."

"People will do business with you for three reasons, in this order of priority. Number one, because they like you. Number two because they are comfortable with you, and comfortable doing business with you. Number three, because they need or can use the product or services that you represent."

In my own mind, I knew that he had those three out of order. Obviously people will buy your product or service first of all because they need it. So for over a year I didn't worry about whether anyone liked me or was comfortable with me. I figured that all I had to do was to expose enough people to our business that needed it and they would become customers. Ignoring my mentor's advice probably cost me thousands of dollars. I talked to hundreds of people who desperately needed what we were offering. Some of them realized it even before I met them, and they still did not do business with me. I finally came to the conclusion that even if they need what you have and can afford it, they won't do business with you if they don't like you, or if they are not comfortable with you for whatever reason.

We spent most of our time looking at cars instead of talking business, but when I left I was excited about getting started so that I could have a car like that one day.

At one point in the next couple of months I got so frustrated with my lack of progress I went to Ralph and said, "Why are all these people so stupid, we have the solution to their problem, we show it to them and they even agree with everything I say, and then they won't act on it. They say that they want to think about it, or they want to talk it over, or check back with us later, and nothing ever comes of it. What's wrong with them, anyway?"

My mentor smiled that knowing smile, and nodded his head like he understood, but then he didn't answer me, instead he changed the subject. So I figured that he didn't know the answer either. After a minute he laughed out loud, and said, "Hey did you ever hear the story about this old boy that was driving down the interstate and his wife called him on the cell phone and said, 'Honey I was worried about you, so I just called to warn you, they said on the radio that some fool is driving the wrong way down interstate sixty-five, so be careful.' The old boy answered her back and said, 'Honey what are you talking about! There are hundreds of them going the wrong way.'

So I laughed at his joke, and said, "Now getting back to these people…"

Then he changed the subject again and said, "Hey, have you ever read Dale Carnegies book *'How To Win Friends and Influence People'*? This world would be a whole lot better if everyone would just read that book and apply the principles to their lives."

Years before I actually had read straight through it, put it down, and never really tried to apply it to my life, but I told him that I agreed with him, the world would be a much friendlier place if everyone else would just do what that book teaches. When I mentioned arguing with a person at work recently he said, "Never argue with, or debate an idiot, he'll pull you down to his level and then beat you with experience."

I think it was the next day as I was reviewing my notes from our meeting that I realized that my mentor had never changed the subject. He had been telling me what I needed to understand in an indirect way. I later found out that it was what he called, teaching in the third person. He could have said, 'Look, stupid, its not all those other people, its you. You're not friendly, your tone of voice is full of sarcasm and ridicule, and you offend people. They think that you are looking down your nose at them and they can tell that you really don't care about them. That's why they don't do business with you.' Instead of being direct and blunt, he taught indirectly, and got me to read a book that helped me to realize for myself what I needed to change.

Sometimes we aren't willing to accept correction from someone we know, but if we read it in a book, written by an 'expert' we will accept it. We're all on our own path to learning, and many times we are not ready to receive the instructions that are given that could change our lives.

The next time I went to see him; we jumped into the car again. We ended up at Rock Harbor Marina, talking as we walked up and down the docks looking at boats of all sizes, from fishing and skiing boats up to one hundred and thirty foot yachts.

I told him that I had learned the Dale Carnegie principles. Even had them memorized.

He said, "Years ago when Betty and I were starting out, my mentor said something that helped me out a lot. He said that 'nothing is learned until it is applied'."

By now I was catching on to the third person teaching, and I caught that one like a slap in the face. Over time I learned that he was right; there is a big difference in having 'read, or heard,' and in having learned what you read, by applying it to your life.

We climbed aboard a couple of the yachts, and sat around like we owned them. What a lifestyle the people must have who really did own them! We sat and talked as we watched the boats come in and out of the harbor.

On many occasions when we were together he wouldn't answer a question directly, he would ask me questions and force me to think through the situation myself, until I had come up with the answer that he would have given. In that way, he taught me to think for myself, and to be able to reason things out. Later in our relationship when we got together, I would say, "This is the problem that I am having... these are the possible solutions that I have been able to come up with.... this is the one that I think is the best... what do you think?

Sitting there on the yacht, he asked a lot of questions and let me talk until I realized that I wasn't getting any questions answered, and asked him about people skills.

He said, "Keep it simple. There are seven things you need to remember and apply, and you'll make friends everywhere you go."

"Number one is to smile. A smile is a universal language. It tells people that you like them, you're their friend, and you mean them no harm. People are attracted to people who smile."

I tried to practice a friendly smile as I watched some small fish jumping in the water. I remember thinking that it sure would be great to have a nice boat to be able to get out on the water.

He said, "Number two, make eye contact. They say that the eyes are the windows to the soul, and people want to know who you really are, so look them in the eye.

If you don't look them in the eye they may get the impression that you have something to hide, or that you don't care about them, or that you aren't being totally honest."

We were looking at a forty-five foot cabin cruiser with teak handrails and very sleek lines. He said, "Picture yourself at the helm. Cruising down the river to the gulf and heading over to the islands, dropping anchor in Dead Man's Bay where Blackbeard the pirate stayed because of its beauty, palm trees swaying in the breeze, beautiful white sand beach, crystal clear, turquoise colored waters, so clear you can see the bottom twenty feet down, snorkeling with your friends and family, can you see it?"

I said, "I can imagine it, but it's hard to believe."

He said, "Belief will come, for now just keep picturing it in your mind."

"The third thing to remember, Tim, is to use a persons name when you are talking to them. People love to hear their name; it is a form of recognition, so use it when you greet them and in your conversation."

"Complimenting people would be the fourth thing to improve your people skills. Look for and find something that you like about them, and make it sincere. People will remember things you say about them for years, so say nice things that they will remember you by. It is even more effective if you say good things about people to someone else, who will tell that person what you said about them."

Note: When I first started hanging around with my mentor, and trying to build a business like he had done, it was very frustrating and I just couldn't seem to get anything going. Several times I had even thought about quitting, I just didn't have any other options available to create a better lifestyle. At one gathering, people were talking about some others who had quit, and as I walked up, Ralph introduced me to some of his friends by saying this, "This is Tim Hendricks, one of my business partners. You couldn't blow him out of this business with three sticks of dynamite!" That comment was made over ten years ago, and I still remember it to this day.

He said, "Number five, you need to touch people. Physical contact is important. In our society, a firm handshake is a friendly greeting. Don't get into a squeeze contest, but let them know that you are there. Did you know that it is a proven fact that newborn babies that are not allowed to have any human contact will digress and eventually die, even if they have every thing else that is necessary for them to grow?

The sad thing is that adults need human contact just as bad as babies; it just isn't quite so obvious. So shake peoples hands, pat them on the back, touch them on the arm, and put your arm around their shoulders. Never do anything improper, but give the ladies a 'shoulder hug', side to side, or lean forward and give them a 'neck hug' and let them know you care about them."

After that, I noticed that Ralph always made people feel good when they came into his presence. He smiled, was the first to reach out his hand, looked them in the eye, and complimented them. You couldn't help feeling better about yourself after being around him. He treated everyone like they were somebody important. He would give the ladies a polite hug, slap the guys on the back, and make anything you had done sound like a great accomplishment.

"The sixth thing would be to watch your tone of voice. If you don't know how you sound to others, carry a recorder with you for a few days and see if you would be attracted or turned off by the tone of voice you use. Your tone can totally change the meaning of a word or a sentence."

"Listen to these three simple words, 'I love you'. With emphasis on 'I', the words would mean that 'I' love you, not Tom, not Sam. 'I' am the one that loves you. With emphasis on 'love', it would mean, I LOVE you, I don't hate you, I don't despise you, I LOVE you. With emphasis on 'you', it would mean, I love YOU, not Sally, not Jane, I love YOU."

"The seventh thing you need to do is to show a sincere interest in the person you are talking to. Do that by asking questions to get them talking and then you just shut up and listen. People love to talk about themselves and their interests, and nobody cares enough to listen to them. So give them your ear and they will love you for it."

After a minute he said, "Conflict between people is inevitable. One of the biggest keys to success is to learn to relate to a wide variety of people and develop the personal skills we've been talking about so that you can competently cope with any conflict you get involved with. Continue to educate yourself. Just reading a book as most people do is not good enough. Education has not taken place unless the mind has matured and emotion has been aroused."

We headed back down the docks and I thought to myself, this is going to be a lot of fun, hanging out with Ralph, looking at boats and things.

"Listen," he said, "you have what it takes to build this business. You can succeed to any level that you choose. Look at the business as an adventure. You never know what is going to happen on a daily basis, but if you are out there chasing your dreams, and you don't quit, they will eventually come true."

I wondered how he knew that I had what it took. For a long time I didn't believe myself that I had what it would take, I was just hoping that I did. All of my friends and family told me that I didn't have what it took and that I would never make it. They knew that I was an extreme loner and wasn't comfortable talking to people. I wanted to believe Ralph, so I told myself that my family and friends didn't know what they were talking about. Ralph had seen thousands of people come into the business, many of them had succeeded and many of them quit. So maybe he could see something in me that I couldn't see myself. In actuality Ralph knew that everyone he worked with had great potential and he did everything he could to encourage him or her to achieve more. I just happened to be one of the few who chose to believe him.

As we were leaving the marina he said, "I've been giving some of my other business associates a challenge. I don't know if you would be interested in participating or not, but you can if you want."

Looking back, he had probably already figured out that I love a good challenge. At that moment I decided that whatever it was, I was going to do it, and hopefully faster, or better than anyone else. It would be a lot of fun. I said, "Sure, what have you got?"

"The challenge, is to go out in public and deliberately use all seven of these techniques on ten different people and call me back with the results of what happens."

I felt a sinking feeling in the pit of my stomach. I thought to myself, this isn't going to be any fun at all. Go out and talk to strangers! For me, this was not going to be easy.

He must have seen me turning white, because he said, "You don't have to do it if you are not up to it; it's just something I have my leaders doing."

Have you ever felt the hair stand up on the back of your neck? Mine was doing it again. If I weren't up to it, I would get myself up to it.

I faked a smile, "No sweat, I'll call you in a few days and let you know what happened."

In the next few days I pushed through my fears and the results were amazing! It helped me to overcome my fears of talking to people because I didn't have to think about what to SAY. I just started out by smiling, greeting people, and asking them a question or complimenting them on something, and if they responded in a friendly way, I asked another question and got them to start talking. Then I just smiled, nodded, listened intently, and asked another question about more details. I found out that people will talk about themselves, and what they are interested in, for hours. They'll tell you their life story, their dreams and goals, likes and dislikes. As I left one guy, he said that I was a great conversationalist and I could come back and talk anytime. I hardly said a word; he had done all the talking!

When I called my mentor back a few days later, I said, "I've figured out how to have more friends. Just meet a lot of people and be their friend first, and many of them will turn into friends."

Ralph said, "That's true, most people are so busy in their lives that they don't have much time for friends, so if you go out of your way to show a sincere interest in other people, you can very quickly become one of their closest friends, and then one day you'll end up owning a nice cabin cruiser like the one we looked at."

I wasn't comfortable talking to people, but for a cabin cruiser, I decided that I would go ahead and do it anyway. (I wasn't comfortable, but I wasn't stupid either.)

Ralph & Betty with U.S. Congressman Jack Kemp

Ralph & Betty with Bart Starr,
World Champion NFL Quarterback and Coach

~ · CHAPTER · ~

FOUR

Late one night at a coffee shop I witnessed an incredible event. After a business meeting, a group of us had gone to the coffee shop and had taken up all the tables in the back of the restaurant. As usual, I was seated with my back to the wall where I could see the door, a habit I had picked up in my younger, less well-mannered days. My mentor was one of the last to come in, so I saw him as he crossed the restaurant and sat down across from me. It was after midnight and some of the local bars were closing, and like a lot of other cities, the local drunkards were staggering in to have some coffee before heading home. As my mentor took his seat, I noticed an old drunken hag come staggering up to the door. It took her a minute to get the door open and stumble inside, supporting herself with the wall as she walked. She was dirty, grimy, and looked as if she lived perpetually in a state of drunkenness. She came straight back to our table, at least as straight as she could, and stopped about three feet behind Ralph, who was in an animated conversation with the other guys at the table, and had not seen her come in. She was obviously not a physical threat, but she was just as obviously

75

ticked off about something, so I was watching her very closely. When she finally spoke, it was kind of a raspy, loud whisper, and her words were very slurred, but she finally got it out. " You sh…sh…shhlammed the door ri…ride in ma face."

Since I was the only one watching her, I was the only one who had heard her, so she stepped forward and tapped Ralph on the shoulder, and as best she could, told him that she was coming in the door right behind him, and that he had slammed the door on her.

Ralph was always aware of what was going on around him, so he knew that it wasn't true, and I knew it wasn't, because he was already seated before she had staggered up to the door.

My temper flared, and my blood started pumping. How dare such a destitute piece of trash accuse such an upright and outstanding person as my mentor of doing that, and to do it in front of his business associates! I was considering coming to his defense, and trying to decide whether I should give her a verbal tongue lashing, or physically drag her back outside and deposit her back into the gutter where she had come from, when Ralph turned his chair around until he was facing her, and even seated, he was almost at eye level with her.

Then his right hand reached out and very gently touched her on the forearm, and in the most gentle and humble tone he said, "I am so sorry, I didn't notice you coming in behind me. I must have been too busy thinking about something else. I would never have let the door close on you if I had seen you coming. Can you forgive me?"

I don't know who was more stunned, she or myself. She had come in looking for a verbal fight, and Ralph's response totally stunned her. You could literally see the fire draining from her eyes and her face.

He said, "I really am sorry, will you please forgive me?"

At that point, I'm not sure who felt like a bigger jerk, her or me. She dropped her eyes, slowly nodded her head, turned and shuffled away.

A few weeks later I asked, "How do you control your emotions?"

He said, "I don't know that I control my emotions. I feel the same emotions that everyone else feels. What I try to do is to control my response to the emotions that I feel. I try to control my attitude, and my actions, and do what is right, regardless of what emotions I'm feeling."

I said, "So how do you do that?"

"I know who I am, and I know where I'm going. I'm a sinner saved by the grace of God, my past has been forgiven, now I'm a child of the King, my future is assured, so why would I allow something happening in the present to upset me?"

He could see that I was struggling with it, so he said, "Zig Ziglar puts it this way; let's say that you are a Dallas Cowboys fan. Let's say that they had won the Super Bowl and you didn't get to see it, so the next day you sit down to watch a video of the game. You already know the end result, because it was on the television news and in the newspapers. At the end of the third quarter would you lose control of your emotions when the other team scored again, putting them ahead by twenty-one points? No! You'd be as cool as a cucumber. You don't know what's going to happen in the fourth quarter, but you know the final score! I know the final score in life; I've read the book. None of us are going to make it out of this world alive, but if we are in a right relationship with God, we have a home in heaven waiting for us."

By now he had figured out that I was referring to the restaurant incident.

He said, "If God has blessed me more than another person, whether with better looks, better health, more intelligence, more material wealth, or whatever, I don't feel like that makes me any better than any other person. It just makes me more thankful. If I see people who are better off than myself, in any way, I don't compare myself to them. Who am I to question God? Besides that, almost all unhappiness is caused by comparison. Whenever you feel unhappy, stop comparing your situation with someone else that you think is doing better than you, and sit down and count your blessings. Write down all the things that you can be thankful for, and before you know it, your whole attitude will have changed.

If you never compare your life with others who have more, and if you are thankful for what you have, your life will be filled with joy, and will be much more satisfying."

A few years later the subject of emotions came up again. We were flying to Hawaii and in route the pilot pointed out Hoover Dam as we were going over the area.

Ralph said, "You're emotions are like water."

I said, "What do you mean?"

He said, "Before the dam was built, the river provided people down river with drinking water, and water to irrigate their crops. But whenever there was a heavy rain, that same river would destroy the crops, destroy homes, and even kill people. Then someone decided to control the flow of the river and built the dam. By controlling the flow of water through the gates, they can provide water to drink, water to irrigate, as well as a beautiful lake where families can come to camp, fish, water ski, or jet ski, or go boating, and it also generates enough electricity to power several major cities. Controlling the flow of water provides a lot of benefits to a lot of people. Your emotions are the same way. You can let them flow freely and whenever there is a flood, or an emotional crisis, your emotions can destroy everything around you. They can ruin your career, your family, your health, and so on. Or you can learn to control your response to the flow of emotions to the benefit of yourself and everyone around you. You can't stop feeling the emotion of anger, but you can choose to control your actions and what you say regardless of what you are feeling. It's not easy, but it can be done with practice"

I remembered another verse that I had heard from my dad's pulpit, 'Be ye angry, and sin not.' I said, "But sometimes you'll get walked on badly if you don't show some anger. You will become somebody's punching bag."

He said, "Look out there. There is nothing more peaceful, calm, or serene than water in a lake, as smooth as glass, that mirrors the surrounding mountains. But there is nothing more deadly than that water if it was suddenly released from that dam holding it. Nothing on earth could stand up to it and survive. The same ingredient, water, can be peaceful or deadly. The same is true of human emotions. What makes them peaceful or deadly is the amount of control.

There may come a time in your life when allowing your emotions to become a tidal wave would be the proper response and you should have the capability to do that. But you have to be in control so that it is your conscious decision whether you respond calmly, or violently. You should never allow your emotions to determine how you act or react."

On another occasion I was telling Ralph about all of the circumstances that were hindering me from building my business. "After I get off work, I come home and have to mow and trim the yard, take out the trash, walk the dog, feed the dog, change the oil in the car or truck, go through the mail, write out checks to pay the bills, watch the news so that I know what the weather will do tomorrow, listen to voicemail messages, eat a quick meal, shower and shave, listen to my wife tell me what all had happened to her that day, and on and on. I don't do all those things every day, but I just can't seem to find time to work at my business. The same seems to be true of others that I am working with. If we could all just change our circumstances, like where we live and the hours we work, then maybe we could put more time into the business."

Ralph told me that most people don't need to change their circumstances; they need to change their habits. Too many people confuse the urgent, with the important. There are things that have to be done in life, like washing clothes, cleaning house, and the things you mentioned. But those things are not important to your future. Things that are vitally important to your future never seem to pop up in your life as being urgent. It's easy to think, 'I don't have to make that call or go see that person right now, I can do it later, because whether I do it right now or not, will not affect my life today.'

So you have to learn to make a list of things that are vital to your future, and a list of things that just have to be done. Then prioritize the list and start at the top with the highest priority. Don't go to the next one until that one is done. Create habits of doing things that are important during prime time. That is the time between when most people get home from work and when they go to bed. Let's say that's from six until ten in the evening. Do all the 'necessary' things before or after prime time. Reserve prime time for doing things that are important to your future.

On another occasion I asked Ralph about men's suits, because a local department store had a special going on. Three suits for a couple hundred dollars.

That is when he taught me the principle of quality, not quantity. His advice was to live by a simple rule, quality not quantity. He said, "Buy half as many, but twice the quality."

He said that if you have a hundred cheap, ill-fitting suits, you always look cheap. If you have just a few good quality suits tailored to fit, you always look like a million bucks. Get a variety of nice silk ties and you can totally change the look with the same suit. The same people won't be seeing you often enough to remember your suit anyway. They will remember the impression you made.

They will either remember, "He dresses nice, looks great", or "Looks like he's wearing someone's hand-me-downs". "Looks like he shops at the Goodwill Store."

So get a dark suit, black, blue, or gray. A few nice quality silk ties with red in them, some white shirts, a black belt, and a good pair of black dress shoes, because black shoes go with anything.

Use the same principle with shoes, belts, ties, and shirts. Just remember, twice the quality, and half the quantity that you can afford, and you'll be good to go.

Ralph & Betty with Danny Gans,
Las Vegas entertainer

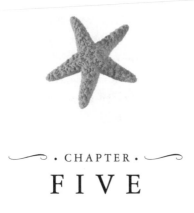

⌐◦ · CHAPTER · ◦⌐

FIVE

At one point in time I finally started doing what he was suggesting I do to create a big income from my new business. I did exactly what he said for me to do, week after week, and two months later, my business income had barely changed. I had called and asked if I was doing something wrong. His response was, "Just keep doing what you are doing." I was very frustrated, and thought that all that effort was for nothing, so I didn't want to keep doing the same thing if it wasn't going to get me anywhere.

I flopped into the seat beside him in the Cadillac, and as we headed to the motorcycle dealership, I voiced my frustration and my complaints about some of the sorry prospects I had encountered lately.

He said, "Some prospects say they are open minded, but we find out that they are confusing it with empty minded."

I said, "I've run into a whole bunch of them that are confused and empty minded, in fact, there just doesn't seem to be any intelligent life on the planet. I'm putting in a lot of effort and not getting any results."

After a long silence, with a concerned look on his face, he said, "I don't believe that God speaks directly to man with an audible voice as he did in Old Testament days. The Bible tells us that he has spoken to us through his son, and we have the Bible in written form to guide us, but I heard a story one time that illustrates a point, about a man that was very weak. Weak and frail physically, weak emotionally, always worried about everything, no self confidence, concerned about what others thought of him, afraid to talk to people, always making excuses about why he didn't accomplish more. He was just a basket case. So he prayed to God, "Lord, help me please!" God came down and said, "Are you just complaining, or will you do what I say?"

The man said, "I'll do whatever you say. I'm ready for a change. You just tell me what to do and I'll do it." Already he felt a boost in his confidence level. God was going to help him overcome his pitiful station in life.

God said, "Good, come over here. Do you see this rock?"

The man was trembling in anticipation of what great things the God of Heaven was going to have him do. He said, "I see it."

The rock was about ten feet tall, fairly round, and must have weighed six or seven tons.

God said, "I want you to push on the rock with all your might, and keep on pushing until I come back."

The man said, "Push?"

"Yes."

"Against the rock?"

"Yes, until I come back," came the answer.

The man was confused, and didn't really understand, but, after all, this was God talking to him. So he took a deep breath, and said, "Okay." And he started pushing. He would push with all his might until he was out of breath, stop to catch his breath, and then push some more. He pushed forward, backward, over handed, underhanded, and sideways with his shoulder.

By evening he was utterly exhausted. He went home and ate a big meal, then dropped into bed and slept like a log. When he awoke, he was stiff and sore from head to toe. He had a big breakfast, and went back the rock and started pushing. Neighbors came by and asked what he was doing. He said, "I'm trying to move this rock." When they asked why, he replied, "This is what God wants me to do." They all told him that he was crazy, and that he would never be able to move the rock by himself. People walked away from him in fits of laughter and started telling others about him. Before long, he was the laughing stock of the community.

"He says that God wants him to move the rock! Ha-ha-ha, what a fool. Why don't you go get a job, or do something useful with your life?" The man just kept pushing, only stopping to catch his breath, eat, sleep, relieve himself, and then push some more. At first the laughter and ridicule bothered him, but then he asked himself, "What if everyone did think he was crazy? God told him to push against the rock, so he must have something really great in mind for him, and maybe this was just a test. So he kept pushing. The taunts began to roll off his back like the beads of sweat pouring off his body in the long hot summer days. Before God had spoken to him he would run inside at the first drop of rain. Now he had something to accomplish, so he pushed in sunshine or in rain. Day after day, week after week he pushed. When the ridicule didn't stop him, the watchers gave him the silent treatment. They would stand around and talk about him, but would not talk to him. If he talked to them, they gave him the cold shoulder and acted as if he didn't exist. Still he persisted. God must be coming back to make something of him at any time.

When the silent, cold shoulder treatment didn't stop him, the spectators began to get curious, mostly when there was no one else around. "This thing that you are doing, do you really think this is what God wants you to do?"

"Yes, absolutely."

"But you've been pushing for months and I can't tell that you've accomplished anything. You are persistent though, I'll give you that."

Some would say, "You haven't moved that rock an inch. How long do you think that God wants you to keep trying?"

Several of the local young men had overheard some young ladies saying that they actually admired him for his persistence, and for continuing to do what he believed in. Wanting some admiration for themselves, they said that they could push on the rock just as good as he could. Some of them would push and push until they got out of breath, and then quit and go home, or someone else would come along and laugh at them, and they were too thin-skinned to withstand the ridicule, so they would stop.

They told the young ladies that they were just going to back off for a while, they had more important things to do right now, they needed to spend some time with their families, but when they got started again, they would really show everyone what they were made of. But no one ever saw them come around again. No one ever really announced that they were quitting; they just gave some lame excuse and faded away.

Finally, the man himself began to doubt, so he sat down and started praying. "God I'm never going to be able to move this rock, no matter how long or hard I push, I can't even budge it."

God's answer came back, "I don't recall telling you that I wanted you to move the rock."

Now the man was really confused. "Well then what was the purpose of having me push against it for all these many months?"

God answered, "Were you not weak and frail physically, mentally, and emotionally, afraid of others opinions, easily swayed in your thinking, unable to find work?"

"Yes."

"And did you not ask me for help?"

"Yes, and all you've had me do is push against this stupid rock!"

God said, "Look at your skin. It is now a beautiful bronze from exposure to the sun, and it is stretched tight over the muscles that ripple beneath it. Look at your arms; your forearms, biceps, and triceps bulge with the muscles that you have developed. Your shoulders can now carry as much of a load as any man in town. Look at your legs; they are as stout as an oak tree. Your jaw is chiseled and firm. Your heart and lungs are strong. And as for your character, you now have the reputation of being one of the most committed, determined, persistent men the town has ever seen.

The opinions of others are like birds chirping in the distance. You are aware of them, but they have zero effect on your attitudes or your actions. You knew that you were doing as I instructed and you did it by faith, not understanding the reason or the purpose. Very few men ever learn to live by faith. There will be many business people who would now like to hire you, or make you a business partner, and many ladies who are looking for a man of your character. You have now developed physical strength, emotional stability, a clear perspective of what it takes to succeed, and strength of character so that you may have a rewarding life whether it be as a career employee, or as an entrepreneur in a business of your own. So go now. You will never move this rock, but with the strength of character you now have, you will be able to move mountains in any chosen field of endeavor."

Ralph finished the story and looked over at me. I was speechless, visualizing myself pushing against the rock for the last two months and not moving an inch. He said, "Just keep doing what you are doing. You cannot always measure the results of your efforts with the human eye. Only looking back, years later, will you be able to see the results of the effort that you are putting forth today. Actually, you will probably never be aware of all of the results of your efforts. Just work like it all depends on you, and pray like it all depends on God."

"Think about how many people's lives the man pushing against the rock may have affected? How many people who came into contact with him may have gone home determined to be more like him, persistent, committed, living by faith, etc. How many lives did those people have an affect on? You're doing the right things. Eventually you will learn to be effective at doing them, and you will have become the kind of person that can do them very effectively, and the kind of person that other people will want to be around."

He laughed out loud and said, "And then someone will put you up on a stage, in the spotlight, and give you a standing ovation and treat you like you are a superstar. That's what they did with Betty and me, and all I did was to push on my rock, this business, until I became who I wanted to be."

He went on, "In life you'll be tempted often by what appear to be shortcuts to getting what you want. Always remember this. Be careful of what you become, in the pursuit of what you want."

I said, "What do you mean?"

He said, "Let's say that you want a million dollars."

"I do."

"So you go out and rob a bank and you have what you WANT, your million dollars, but what have you BECOME?"

"A bank robber," I said.

"And what happens to bank robbers," he asked.

"Bad stuff."

"Which is not what you want, so be careful of what you become in the pursuit of what you want. Some people want to be happy so they try a shortcut called drugs, or alcohol. They not only ruin their own lives, and the lives of those around them, but what do they become?"

I said, "Brain dead alcoholics or drug addicts."

He said, "You need to understand something Mister. In the pursuit of what you want, what you become is far more important than what you get. In the end, a person is known only by the impact and the influence they have had on others. One of these days they are going to put you in a box and drop you down into a hole and then they are going to shovel dirt in your face. Then they are going to go home and eat fried chicken and potato salad and talk about you. And you are the one that determines what they say about you when you are gone, by the manner in which you live your life. If you aren't careful of what you are becoming, your talent can take you where your character can't sustain you."

It was kind of morbid visualizing your own funeral and then wondering what people would be saying about you after you were gone. Luckily we arrived at the Harley dealership and the conversation turned to fun and excitement.

We sat on some beautiful Harley Davidson's with custom paint jobs, and chrome everywhere. I would definitely be the big shot on the block with a Harley! And according to Ralph, all I had to do to get one was to keep pushing on my rock!

Since all I could think about was the rock and people shoveling dirt in my face and talking about me, I went home and started pushing, determined to whine and complain less, to learn whatever lessons were in store from pushing my business relentlessly ahead, and determined to treat people around me better. Ralph said that you needed to have at least six friends when it was all over because it took six to carry the box.

Ralph, daughter Susan, and Betty with Norman
Schwarzkopf U.S. Army General, ret.

SIX

We were out looking at houses again. As we were going through a home that was under construction, I mentioned to Ralph that a guy I had known in college had died from a heart attack at the age of thirty-five.

Ralph said that he was sorry, and then he said, "To die of heart attack at that age, I would say he was overweight, didn't exercise, didn't take vitamins or food supplements, drank alcohol, and smoked."

I said, "Four out of five. He didn't drink. How did you know all that?"

As he often did, he answered my question with a question. "How long does the normal car last before it goes to the junk yard?" By now I knew that he wasn't changing the subject, so I stayed with him.

I said, "My guess would be five to ten years."

He said, "Most of the commercial airplanes you see flying today are thirty or forty years old. How come they are still flying and cars are dead in five to ten years?"

"Good question," I said. "I've never thought about that before."

Then he explained that there are no laws on maintaining your personal vehicle. The Federal Aviation Administration has strict guidelines for maintaining aircraft. First of all they keep detailed records, then they have scheduled maintenance, like an oil change and lube job on your car. If the manufacturer says to change the oil every three thousand miles, radiator flush every fifty thousand miles, or whatever and you don't do any of it, your car will break down sooner, but no one cares. If you have an airplane that is scheduled for maintenance, it doesn't leave the ground until it is done. They also know the lifespan of every part on that plane. If it has a lifespan of one year, the FAA requires that it be replaced every six months, or whatever they decide. So all the working parts of an airplane are continually being replaced. The only thing forty years old is the shell, and the non-working parts. It always has the fluids it needs and the new parts it needs to function properly.

He said that the human body is like an aircraft, or a car. It was designed and engineered to work at peak performance as long as it is cared for and has all the pieces and parts it needs to function properly.

It needs clean air and water just like a car motor. It needs a steady fuel supply taken in by mouth, digested in the stomach and intestines, and converted into energy for the body to burn and eliminate the waste, just like a cars gasoline fuel injection system, manifold, cylinders, exhaust, muffler, etc.

He asked, "Are you with me?"

"Yes, that makes sense."

He went on to explain that the body also has need of parts and fluids that would compare to windshield washer fluid, brake fluid, transmission fluid, antifreeze, gaskets, o-rings, seals, flanges, etc. He called those things vitamins and food supplements and said that they are contained in some of the food we eat, but because most of the ground has been depleted of these nutrients and all of our foods are processed with heat, chemicals, radiation, preservatives and such, what little nutrients that may have been there are stripped out of it before it ever reaches us. Some are more important than others, just like in a car.

He asked, "Would you rather run dry of windshield washer fluid or brake fluid?"

I said, "I see what you mean."

"Either one could cause an accident, but one is more likely to cause problems sooner. The same is true with the human body." He went on to describe the vital necessity of vitamins, minerals, and herbs, and the function of each in the human body. Essentially, never taking food supplements would be like buying a car and driving it for years, without ever doing any kind of maintenance, without ever changing fluids, or adding fluids. The body will wear out much faster, the same as a car would.

Some vitamins can be stored in the body, others cannot, so they need to be replenished daily. Whenever the body needs some vitamin A, it sends a signal or a runner to pull it off the shelf and take it to where it is needed. If it isn't there, the body part or organ will continue to function as well as it can without it. But over an extended period of time, it causes more and more deterioration and breakdown. When one body part isn't functioning at full capacity, it has a detrimental effect on other body parts, causing them to wear out faster. Cells of your body are continually dying and being replaced by new cells. But when the vitamins and minerals aren't there, the new cells are not as strong as the old cells dying off. So the body becomes weaker and more susceptible to injury and illness. Virtually every cell in your body will be replaced every eleven or twelve months. So if you eat moderately, exercise regularly, and take vitamins, minerals, herbs, and supplements, you will continue to have a strong, healthy, vibrant body into old age.

Overeating, not exercising, smoking, drinking alcohol, and taking drugs, whether legal or illegal, will all have a detrimental effect on your body.

Sooner or later we are all going to die. Giving your body what it needs and avoiding things that destroy it raise your odds tremendously of having a long, healthy life.

He finished by saying, "I recommend that everyone read books about how the body works, and the role of vitamins, minerals, and food supplements in your diet."

Ralph taught a very simple way to stay healthy. Eat less, exercise more. If you are overweight then you are probably eating too much and taking in more than your body is burning. So eat less and your body will start to burn the fat that is stored. Exercise more, and your body will burn more fat, faster. (There are some cases where a medical condition exists that will complicate matters, but from my own observations most people could stand to eat a little less and to exercise a little more. Check with your doctor before making any dramatic changes to your lifestyle.)

As we were going through a beautiful log home and admiring the excellent craftsmanship, I said, "I've noticed that when we are around your mentors, that you don't talk much. You ask questions, and then shut up. Is there a specific reason for that?"

He said, "Absolutely. When I am talking, I'm just verbalizing things I already know. When I'm around people that I want to learn from, the only way I can learn something new is to ask questions and then listen. God gave us one mouth and two ears, and I think that we should use them in that proportion."

I made a note to follow that advice and I also got some great ideas for the log mansion I decided to build one day. A massive rock fireplace would be wonderful to have in the great room that was open all the way to the ceiling on the second floor. I would like one entire wall of glass to look out over the countryside. I decided that I wanted a huge antler chandelier hanging above the great room and some antler floor lamps. Western lodge type furnishings would suit me. I would also have several sofas, to be able to seat lots of friends. A huge master bedroom with a king size aspen log canopy bed, and log furniture, separate walk-in closets. My wife is always saying that she has nothing to wear. For years I've wondered what all that stuff in the closet is for. All I know for sure is that it takes a big closet to hold all of that 'nothing'. Separate sinks in the master bath, a big Jacuzzi tub, a separate shower, and a laundry chute which would drop the dirty clothes straight into the laundry room, where a maid would do the laundry, and the next time I saw them, they would be clean and folded in my dresser drawer, or hanging in my closet. A floor drain in the center of the laundry room floor so that the house wouldn't flood, in case the washer hose burst. Lots of skylights in the roof to lighten the place up. An office on the highest level with lots of windows to be able to see in every direction. I'd like a log desk and filing cabinet with antler drawer pulls. A bathroom for every bedroom as well as an extra, or two. (I've seen homes with one bath and a two-car garage, which doesn't make much sense to me. I've never had to wait on a garage.) The home would have to be built on a solid foundation and be built to last, because with all the vitamins and minerals I would be taking, I might live to be a hundred and twenty years old!

Daughter Susan, son Kevin, Ralph,
Betty with the Oak Ridge Boys

~~o · CHAPTER · o~~

SEVEN

I don't know who came up with the idea for a 'Warriors Weekend' but it was an experience like nothing I had ever experienced before in my life. Essentially it was a weekend retreat for men who had been out pursuing their dreams, getting outside of their comfort zone, and making things happen, (warriors), while other males sat at home and complained about their pitiful lot in life.

We headed out Friday afternoon for the lake, several hours away, where the leaders had rented sixty-foot long houseboats for the weekend. There were about 60 men who had qualified to come and so three houseboats were rented. There were enough beds to sleep about twelve per boat and the rest carried sleeping bags. I didn't know there were things that floated that were that nice. They were nicer than any apartment I had ever lived in. They even had a six-person hot tub on the roof. Some of the guys brought their boats along and went fishing, some went water skiing, some jumped off the roof to go swimming, and some stayed inside and watched sports on television. Basically you could do whatever you wanted to do from Friday evening through Sunday afternoon. Throughout the day the leaders would sit down here or there and guys would gather around and start asking questions.

I think everyone there agreed that it would be wonderful to have the time and the money to be able to take their family on a houseboat vacation, or even to own one so that you could 'get away' from the hassles of life whenever you needed to. There just seems to be something that refreshes your spirit when you are cutting across the water with the wind blowing in your face, and the sun shining down and shimmering off the water like a thousand diamonds glittering on a dark blue velvet cloth.

We found a very private island and pulled the houseboats into the bank side by side. Cooking was done on the gas grills. Some of the guys thought that this was roughing it, having to sleep on the floor in a sleeping bag and having only one bathroom for all those guys. Having spent many nights alone, out in the woods, sleeping on the cold, damp ground, and cooking over a fire, I considered this to be living in luxury.

We thought that the main purpose of the trip was to give us a chance to be around our leaders and mentors for an entire weekend. By the end of the weekend some of us had come to the conclusion that the leaders purpose was to get us away from our wives so that they could take off the velvet gloves and tell us man-to-man, with no fluff, what we needed to be doing to make the business work, and to become real men, without our wives there to elbow us. It was kind of like a mental boot camp. They talked about values, principles, character, integrity, courage, bravery, manhood, and doing what is right; all the things that are left out of the teaching process in our 'politically correct' society. Some of the men brought their teenage sons along, and the biggest response from them was, "This is great, we've never heard anybody talk about this kind of stuff before."

In the evening when things began to settle down the leaders would sit around the fire and talk, or answer questions. They talked late into the night, and early into the next morning. Guys were gathered all around, some sitting on a very steep hill. One guy fell asleep and came rolling down the hill about two o'clock in the morning. A lot of questions came up on a lot of different topics and I didn't write down all the questions so I'll just give you many of the responses and discussions that I wrote down. Many of the questions would not have come up in mixed company, many of them about how to get along with spouses who didn't like their husbands building a business on the side, or things of that nature.

In response to one question Ralph said, "First of all, if you don't believe in the Bible, you have problems that can't be solved, because you have no standard to tell you what should, or shouldn't be done. If you do accept that the Bible is God's word, the answers are there. God made man the head of the house and he gave him the responsibility of providing for those within his house. He didn't say that you should provide well for your household if you have your wife's permission to do so. If you have realized that your job, career, or profession is not going to give you the kind of income and time that you need to take care of your family the way that you feel they should be provided for, and you have figured out that this business could provide that, then you should make the decision to move ahead and do what needs to be done because it is your responsibility and you will be held accountable. That does not mean that you should run roughshod over your wife or her feelings. You should always treat your wife with love and respect as the Bible teaches. Usually if you will sit down with her and communicate to her why you feel the way you do, that will solve a lot of the problems. Men simply don't talk to their wives as much as they should. Women like to feel that they are involved and they like to know why things are being done. If you will make them a part of the decision making process they will usually be good team members and do everything they can to help out.

However, from time to time we see a wife who won't support her husbands business, for whatever reason, and my question to the husband is this; would you feel like you would have to get your wife's permission in order to go to work every morning if she didn't like your job or your profession? Most men say 'no' to that because they feel that they have to go to their job to support their family. Well, some men feel just as strongly that they need to build a solid business in order to support their family."

I think that Ralph had figured out that some of the guys were not getting better results because they would not overcome their fears, and they were essentially trying to blame their failure on their wives.

He continued, "On the other hand, if the husband says he is going to do something, is spending time away from her and the kids, spending money going here and going there, and yet he is not doing the actual work of building a business, then she has a right to complain because he is not doing what he said he was going to do, he is just treating the business like a hobby. So try everything you can to get your wife's support, but if she just decides to be a little stinker and not fulfill her marriage vows, then you need to be a man. Take off the pantyhose, put your pants on that zip up the front, and go ahead and build the business. I've never seen a woman yet who wouldn't come around to his way of thinking once they see that the man has made a decision, is sticking with it, getting results, the checks are coming in with comma's in the numbers, and at the same time his attitude toward her is improving."

"If you want your wife's support, start building the business fast. If you don't melt the axle, building the business fast, no one will notice. If you do burn it up, everyone will notice. Develop the courage to overcome your fears. Have the strength to do what needs to be done. Courage attracts attention, strength demands respect."

"If you want to have the respect of your wife, as well as of other people, you have to do more than the ordinary guy. A dog can eat, sleep, work, play ball, have sex, and watch television. Ordinary men today live to do just those six things. So what is the difference in them and animals? Men were created with the capacity to dream, to plan, and to take action to make their dreams come true, so show the world that you are more than an animal, by doing something more than animals do."

"Wives should make the home a safe harbor that the husband looks forward to coming home to; home should not be considered the place where the wicked taskmaster lives, that the husband dreads coming home to. Home should be where a man is appreciated for his efforts, if nothing else. If a woman wonders why her husband likes to work late or go out and do things after work, she should stop and take a look at the atmosphere that she creates that the man has to come home to. On the other hand, men should take a close look at how they are treating their wives when they come home. Don't come in and dump all over her about how bad your day was and take out your anger on her. Ask her how her day was and then just listen and let her talk. Compliment her on how she is handling everything and give her a hug. She should look forward to you coming home, not dreading it.

Someone asked how you keep a positive attitude in a bad situation. His response was, "Develop the attitude that thorn bushes have roses, not that rose bushes have thorns. Life is not always going to be a bed of roses. Life is hard. Bad things happen. But if you will look for the good in every situation, you can usually find a benefit hidden in every problem."

"The best helping hand you will ever receive is at the end of your wrist."

"Decisions are made on emotions, and logic is used to back up the decision." He gave one example of a husband whose family was growing, and because of the children, they had decided to buy a mini-van. They had analyzed the situation and decided that a mini-van would be a practical, economical, logical choice in vehicles. They saved up their money and then the husband went to look at mini-vans. He wasn't real excited about the prospects of driving one, but he knew logically it was the right thing to do. While at the dealership he spotted a bright red pre-owned corvette for about the same price as the mini-van. He knew that it was not really a practical option, but he decided to test drive it just for the heck of it. The rush of emotions, the adrenaline, the power, the excitement, the thrill, the prestige! When he got home he explained the purchase of the corvette to his wife logically. If you buy a new mini-van it depreciates in value by about thirty percent when you drive it off the lot and it will continue to go down in value until its just a piece of junk to be hauled off. I've also heard that because of the way they are constructed, if it rolls over, it splits in half killing everyone inside. This corvette will continue to increase in value year after year, in fact we may be able to sell it one day and pay for one child's college education. Ralph said, "We recommend finding things that get you excited, that get your blood flowing, that give you a rush, and use that energy to overcome all the obstacles to building a big business. Then when the money comes in let logic take over. Do what should be done, what is responsible given your financial position. Put the money into the business and into paying off your bills before you go off and buy something on emotion."

Someone asked what he meant when he talked about lifestyle. "Lifestyle is when your banker, your accountant, and your florist know you by your voice and greet you by your first name. Last week I called American Airlines and the reservations agent recognized my voice. Lifestyle is having the time and the money to do just about anything you want to do; the hardest thing being to decide between all the options."

When asked about people's animosity about individuals in this business he said, "Being first in anything creates jealousy, hatred, envy, slander, fear, and anger. That which is great will live, in spite of the attack, in spite of being assailed."

"All great religions have grown under great pressure, in the caves and in houses; and die slow comfortable deaths in the cathedrals and church buildings. Most of the people who become wealthy in this country, come out of poverty, not from the comfortable middle class."

"A champion doesn't become a champion the day he gets the recognition or the award. A champion is a champion the first day he rolls out of bed and goes out into the cold, alone, and starts running. But you have to persist. Many people start, but few people finish what they start. People are recognized and rewarded for what they finish, not for what they start."

When asked how he would respond when someone asks him, "What do you do?" he said, "I tell them, 'I pull Ostrich heads out of the ground.' When an Ostrich gets scared it will stick it's head under the sand, or under cover much like people do. Most people know that what they are doing isn't working financially but thinking about the future and what is going to happen to them if they keep doing what they are doing scares them, so they stick their head in the ground and act like everything will be alright if they just ignore the problem. I pull people's head out of the ground and show them the facts of life and what they need to do to get ahead financially, and many of them say, 'Oh, my Gosh!' and stick their heads back into the ground, which leaves something else sticking up in the air. Ninety five percent of the people who reach the age of sixty-five will be dependent on welfare, relatives, or still having to work, and it's not because they are lazy. Most of them worked five or six days a week for their whole life. It's because they refused to look down the road to see where they were headed. They simply failed to develop a plan that would provide for them when they wanted to stop working. Success requires no explanations, and failure permits no alibis."

"The opposite of success is indecision. If you don't decide to do something to take care of yourself and your family after you stop working, then you have chosen to end up in the majority who can't even support themselves with any dignity later in life."

"The biggest reason that most men fail is that they never learn to take personal responsibility for their actions. Almost all men want more authority, more respect, and recognition. Mediocre men want authority but not accountability, respect without accomplishment, and recognition for something they did years ago in their 'glory days'. Great men make themselves accountable to people they respect. They know that authority comes hand in hand with responsibility and they are willing to accept it. Great men only expect recognition for what they are accomplishing now. Maturity does not come with age but with acceptance of responsibility. Manhood begins with the acceptance of responsibility for your own actions. You are where you are based on decisions you have made. If you don't like where you are in life, then make a decision to change. You are the only one who can make that decision for yourself. If your spouse could make it for you, she already would have. If I could make it for you, I would have too. If you want respect, admiration, wealth, and all the rest of it, you have to make the decision to pay the price and to do what it takes. If it is not your decision, then when the time comes to hit the pavement on a cold rainy day, you won't move."

Someone brought up challenges and said they felt like they were up to their necks in poop (challenges). Ralph said, "If you take a perfectly good seed and put it out on the concrete it has no challenges, but it will never grow. Drop a pile of poop on it, soak it with rain, let the sun beat down on it, (lots of challenges) and it will begin to grow. Poop is what makes stuff grow. You just have to grow through it. If you are going through a lot of crap that you don't like, just don't stop, keep going.

"Many men pray for wealth. When you pray for wealth, the Lord doesn't just drop the money into your lap without any effort on your part. In response to your prayer He will give you opportunity.

You have to grab the opportunity and do the work, and then you get the wealth. Many men pray for wisdom, expecting the Lord to just implant it into their brain, or speak to them directly, but in response to a prayer for wisdom he gives you problems and challenges. Studying his Word to learn how to overcome those problems and challenges will give you wisdom."

"Every morning when we wake up we stand at the fork of the road. We can choose to do the same thing we have always done, which brings us through a twenty-four hour circle back to the same place we were before, or we can choose to get better by doing something different. We can deliberately break out of our pattern that has not taken us to where we want to be in life. We can read a good book, listen to an audio recording, watch a video, or we can associate with more successful people in order to learn from them. Tomorrow you will have the same choice to make. If you keep doing the same thing, then you have already experienced the high point of your life, because nothing is going to get better without doing something different. Every morning I wake up and decide to get better. I decide to do something to move forward towards accomplishing my purpose in life, and if you are going to experience success in your lifetime, you will have to do the same thing. You have to learn to be productive, not just busy."

"Being productive in life gives you dignity. It maximizes your manhood. Many of the people who have inherited great wealth never found a purpose in life and ended up as drunkards or drug addicts because they spent all their time seeking pleasure for themselves. Those who learn the value of being productive and of helping others, or of making a contribution, are in a position to do a great amount of good because of their wealth and positions of influence."

"The more wealthy you become, the more influence you achieve, the more you will want to spend time with people who care about things that matter. It has been said that little minds talk about other people, average minds talk about things, and great minds talk about ideas that matter, that can make a difference. Albert Einstein turned down fifty thousand dollars for a fifteen-minute interview. He said that he would rather talk to two or three people who understood him than to talk to a million who didn't."

"Napoleon Hill said that over five hundred of the most successful men this country has ever known told him that their greatest success came just one step beyond the point where it looked as if they had been defeated. So when it looks as if all is lost, take a deep breath and charge forward."

Obviously I cannot relate everything that was discussed over an entire weekend, so let me just say that two days with people who think on a higher level than you can help you to change your thinking from where it is, to the kind of thinking that will take you anywhere you want to go in life.

Two days on a vessel worth a quarter of a million dollars on a beautiful lake nestled between the mountains will also change the way you think about just staying home and cleaning out the garage during your annual vacation time!

Tim, Ralph, Anna and Betty

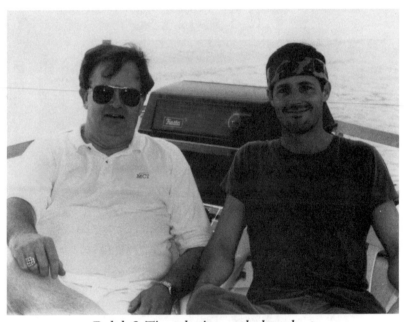

Ralph & Tim relaxing on the houseboat
at Warrior's Weekend

⌒◦ · CHAPTER · ⌒◦

EIGHT

When our Warrior Weekend was over Ralph and I were sitting on the back end of the houseboat headed back across Cumberland Lake. I was wearing an old green army tee shirt, had a camouflage bandana around my head and two days growth of beard. Not exactly the image of success, but more comfortable than I had felt in a long time. Still, I just couldn't seem to get a handle on what I needed to do to be successful. As we cruised across the water I said, "I just don't know if I'll ever get this business put together, I just don't seem to have what is necessary to make it work."

He was looking out across the water, and without hesitation he said, "Only the invisible is necessary."

I turned and stared at him and waited for more explanation, but there was none forthcoming, so I said, "Run that by me again."

He turned and looked me right in the eye and said very slowly and distinctly, "Only the invisible is necessary."

I didn't have a clue what that meant, so I asked him.

He said, "I think that you are frustrated because you are focused on the physical, the material, the things you can see, touch, and feel. Those things are not important."

I could see the sunlight shimmering across the water, I touched the rail and felt the vibrations of the boat beneath me, I felt the spray of the water. I saw a friend step out the back door and snap a picture of us. I said, "So what is important?"

"The things you can't see, touch, or feel."

"Like what?"

He leaned back in his chair and looked at me through his sunglasses as if he were trying to figure out how to explain something to me that was over my head. "Imagine that you are a farmer. In the spring you go out and plant your seed, water it, and fertilize it. Would you then go out every day to watch it grow and worry about it?"

"No."

"Why not? How do you know that it will grow?"

"Well, because people have been planting seeds for thousands of years, and if the seed gets water and sunshine, it will grow."

He said, "But how do you *KNOW* that it will?"

Well, I guess that you don't *KNOW* that it will, you just have faith that if you do what others have done, you will get the same results."

He jumped forward in his seat, *"FAITH?* What is that, show it to me, let me feel it."

I looked at him like he was crazy, "I can't show it to you, it's like, well it's uhh… umm… it's invisible."

He said, "It's invisible. Is it necessary?"

I had to think about it, "Well, yes, because if you didn't have faith, you wouldn't plant the seed, or water it, or fertilize it."

He sat back in his chair, "So as a farmer, you would just do the work that a farmer is known to have to do, and have faith that the crops would grow?"

"Yes."

He said, "What about all the bad things that can happen to

destroy a crop. Flood, drought, insects, wind, hail, fire, etc. how do you go on, knowing all the things that could happen?"

I shrugged my shoulders, "I don't know. I guess you just hope none of those things happen."

Again he jumped forward, "*HOPE?* Show me that, let me see it."

I said, "You can't see hope either, it's....it's invisible too."

He said, "Hope is described as desire with the expectation of getting what you desire. But is hope necessary?"

I said, "Well, yes, I don't see how you could go on without hope."

He said, "Did you know that it has been proven that you can live for thirty days without food, three days without water, three minutes without air. But you cannot live three seconds without hope? That is a scientific fact. People have jumped off high-rise buildings to commit suicide, and the autopsies prove that they were dead before they hit the ground! On two occasions in World War Two a pilot jumped out of his burning airplane from over twenty thousand feet without a parachute and lived. One of them didn't even have any broken bones. How could that be? The truth of the matter is that as soon as the person committing suicide jumped, he gave up all hope of living, and he died instantly, long before he hit the ground. The pilots may have had unique circumstances, like a snowy slope, or very soft ground, which made it possible to survive, but they maintained a hope of living, otherwise they also would have died before impact. But I still don't understand why you as a farmer would go out to the field and work from before daylight until after dark." He leaned back in his seat, "Why on earth would you do that?"

I said, "I guess, because you have a wife and kids to feed and you want to be able to provide for the people you love."

"*LOVE?*" he shouted. "What is that, show it to me, and let me touch it."

As I leaned back in my seat, and stared across the water without seeing, I could remember sitting on the front pew of the church building as I was growing up. The pews were cushioned, the carpet was maroon, and the walls were paneled three feet up from the floor, and then painted white to the ceiling. My dad was in the pulpit finishing up one of his favorite sermons… 'Faith, Hope, and Love, and the greatest of these is love…'

I looked back at my mentor and he was smiling from ear to ear. I said, "It's invisible, and yes it is necessary, because that is what keeps you going when things aren't going the way you want them to."

He said once again, "Only the invisible is necessary."

I said, "So, let me think out loud. If you have faith, then you will be persistent and continue on, in spite of all the visible evidence, the things you can see that make it look as if you will never make it. As long as you have hope for a better future, you won't give up and quit. You'll keep moving forward, trusting or expecting that things will eventually get better. If you have love for God, you'll work as if you were working for God and an eternal reward, and what material rewards you get, or don't get, are really irrelevant. If you love your family, or others, you will push through all the struggles, trials, and challenges because your loved ones are more important than the things you can see, or feel; like the laughter of others, the criticism and the ridicule of people around you, your fear of failure, or your fear of other people. So if you have faith, hope, and love, nothing on earth can stop you from achieving whatever you set out to do, except death. And even that won't keep you from your ultimate goal."

His smile told me that even if I didn't understand it all yet, I was at least on the right track.

He said, "Everything that you can see with the eye came from something that you can't see. A person may have a great idea, but it is invisible. Another person may have a big dream, but that is also invisible. But everything that you can see with the eye, everything that exists in the physical realm existed first in the invisible realm of the mind. Everything that has ever been invented was a thought, before it became reality. So what most people perceive as being 'reality' is really just the outward expression of something that already existed in the mind, or what we might call 'invisible reality'. Just because your ideas or dreams haven't come through to the physical world yet, does not mean they never will. It takes time and effort. So you have to hold on tight to your dreams, you have to feed and nourish your ideas, you have to believe that things will come to pass that you cannot yet see with the eye. See it in your mind, visualize it, picture it, and then work toward making your visible world conform to the invisible picture in your mind. If you hold the picture in your mind long enough with enough intensity and emotion, and if you maintain your faith, your hope, and your dreams, if you are willing to work, willing to learn, and willing to do things that may be uncomfortable at first, then eventually what is invisible will become visible, and you will have what you want out of life. Helen Keller said that the greatest things in the world can't be seen with the eyes, they have to be felt in the heart. So, if you can learn to 'see' the invisible in your minds eye, or feel it in your heart, then you will be able to accomplish that which people of no vision would consider impossible."

On the way back I was calculating how big a business I needed to build, to be able to get a houseboat like this. Then I started picturing making it happen in my mind. I mentally started seeing myself becoming very effective at doing the things that it would take to be successful. I could see myself overcoming the obstacles and achieving the victory. I started succeeding in my mind, choosing to believe that success that could be seen by others would come later.

I decided that I needed to get out on the water at least twice a month. For me it would be very relaxing and refreshing. It would be a business expense of course, since I would be bringing business associates out for training and motivation.

When I started talking to friends and acquaintances about a houseboat they all thought I was crazy, and asked how in the world I thought I could ever afford something like that. They said I didn't have the necessary education to have that lifestyle; I didn't have the necessary high paying job to be able to buy one. But that didn't bother me; I knew the secret. Only the invisible is necessary.

Ralph & Betty with Mike Ditka, NFL player and Coach

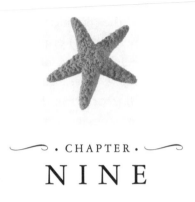

⌒◦ · CHAPTER · ◦⌒

NINE

I had called and asked for some time with my mentor and we were now sitting in the Vanderbilt Plaza Hotel restaurant. The waiters wore tuxedo's, soft piano music was playing, white table cloths on the tables, and I couldn't figure out why anyone would need that many forks and spoons for one meal. I was coordinated enough to eat all five courses with the same fork. Since there were no prices on the menu, I was glad that Ralph had mentioned to the waiter to put everything on his bill. This was the first restaurant where I had ever eaten that didn't call chicken or beef, chicken or beef. It was cordon bleu and fancy names I couldn't even pronounce, but the food was excellent and the service was wonderful. I usually ate where the menu was on the wall and they threw your food at you in a paper bag.

After we had ordered, I said, "We've been working at the business for a while and it is going better than before, but I just can't see how we will ever have the lifestyle that you have."

Ralph said, "It really comes down to three simple words, <u>be</u>, <u>do</u>, and <u>have</u>. Before you can have the trinkets that we have, you have

117

to do what we did to build the business. Before you can do what we did, you have to become the kind of person who can do them effectively. Being comes before doing, and doing comes before having. So if you want what we have, focus on becoming what we are. What we are is more important than the trinkets that we have.

I said, "What do you mean by trinkets?"

He said, "Trinkets are material things. This ring I wear has twenty diamonds, each over half a carat. Betty's five-carat diamond solitaire, my Gucci watch that is several steps up from a Rolex, the Cadillac, the motor coach, custom suits, and designer dresses are all just trinkets. They aren't important, they are just stuff. Don't get me wrong, I enjoy having nice stuff, but all of the material stuff is just the rewards of becoming who we wanted to be, and for accomplishing what we set out to accomplish."

I was looking at Betty's five-carat solitaire that looked a lot like a Volkswagen headlight. "Trinkets?"

He said, "In the hierarchy of human needs, air, water, food, clothing, and shelter are important. Once you have those taken care of, you can start thinking about other things. You'll find that the more people you can be of service to, the more rewards you will receive from life. If you are not satisfied with your income, figure out how you can be of greater service to more people, and your income will go up. As your income grows, the quality of your food, clothing, shelter, and transportation will get better. But what is really important to both Betty and I, is our relationship with God, our relationship with each other and with our kids, our influence in the church and in the community, the respect of people that we respect, and accomplishing our purpose in life. What we have found, is that if your chosen purpose in life is in line with God's will, and you work diligently towards accomplishing your purpose, you'll get all of the basic necessities of life, as well as all of the trinkets you desire along the way. So the trinkets, or material things that we have, were never the goal. They were just by-products of successfully fulfilling our purpose."

"How do you know what your purpose in life is?"

He said, "It's up to each individual to determine what they want to accomplish in life. If you don't know, I would suggest first of all that you study the Bible. It's kind of like an owners manual for human beings, a trouble-shooting guide. If you are having problems with your car, you go to the owner's manual to determine what the problem is, and how to fix it. Or you go to a mechanic who is very familiar with the manual already and ask his advice. The Bible has the answers to all human problems. So study the Bible, or go to someone who is very familiar with it, and who has their life in order, and talk to them. If it isn't clear to you, then just pick a purpose, an ultimate goal, or a mission and start working towards it. Usually, your purpose is tied to something that you feel passionate about. Most people don't realize that there is a purpose for their existence, so they go through life just existing from day to day. They try to do things that will make themselves happy, or buy things to make themselves happy. They never realize the feeling of accomplishment that you get from doing what you have set out to do, and from becoming the kind of person that you set out to become. One of the greatest joys in life comes from helping others, but most people are so self centered they never take their eyes off themselves long enough to help someone else. So they never get to feel that deep down joy and satisfaction that comes from helping someone else, with no thought of reward for themselves."

He went on, "I don't know that God has a different specific purpose in mind for every single person on earth, but I believe that we were all created for a purpose. I think that we are all here to serve God and to keep his commandments, to serve our fellow man, and to live our lives in such a way that our lives will bring glory to God. We can each choose our occupation or what type of business to pursue, but I believe that no matter what we do in life that is good, that brings attention to ourselves, that we should use that opportunity to give God the glory. We should use whatever influence we have to point people towards our heavenly father."

As we sat through the different courses of the meal I brought up another subject that was bothering me. "I know that experience is the best teacher, but at the rate I'm going I'll never have enough experiences to learn all the things I need to know to be successful."

He said, "That is why we have the system that you are involved in. It will teach you how to build the business, as well as to help you to develop business owner mentality and become the kind of person that can build a business successfully. It is the most efficient and professional business education and training program available in the world, and it has helped thousands of people to get their financial freedom. That system includes audio recordings, video's, books, training seminars, weekend conventions, voicemail system, newsletters, professional quality literature and business building tools, as well as a personal mentor to give you one on one help."

Before I could even ask a question he said, "You may ask the same questions I did when I got started in a business of my own. Why do I need all this stuff? So let me just touch on the system, and why you need it. It's real simple. You need the system because no one has ever succeeded in this business long term, without participating in the entire system. It allows you to learn through all of your senses and emotions, not just one sense. A friend of mine named Bert says that it's just like a cake recipe, if you leave one ingredient out, you don't get the results that you wanted. So you have to participate in every ingredient whether you understand why it is in the recipe or not. The more senses that are affected the more quickly and easily you learn. Some people don't like to read, others may not like attending conventions, etc. but when they try to learn through only one or two methods, they just never do get everything they need to be successful."

I said, "But all that training stuff costs money. In fact I've heard of people buying franchises, or business development systems, or stuff like this and then failing in business, and then they tried to sue the people who sold them the training material and the people who produced it."

Ralph said, "Do the ingredients of a cake cost money?"

"Yes."

"If you bake the cake, and you and your family enjoy eating it, were the ingredients worth the money?"

"Yes."

"If you buy the ingredients, with the recipe on the back, put them on a shelf, and never use them, whose fault is it that you never enjoy eating the cake; your fault, the fault of the manufacturer of the ingredients, or the fault of the store who sold them to you?"

I said, "I guess it is yours, since you had the ingredients and you had the recipe and you just didn't do anything with it."

He said, "That is right, so if you don't bake a cake, and the ingredients become worthless, are you going to sue the manufacturer of the ingredients because you never did get to eat cake? Some people would say, 'That's the stupidest thing I've ever heard in my life.' But people go into business and do that all the time. Ninety-nine percent of the time, it never gets to court, or gets thrown out when it does go to court because the judge knows that the lack of results is the fault of the individual."

I told him that I still didn't really understand how all those meetings were going to help me build a business.

He said, "Do you understand how electricity works?"

I said, "No, not really."

"So when you go home at night, do you just sit in the dark, or do you light candles, or what?"

I said, "No, I just flip the switch and turn the lights on."

"Who taught you to do that?"

I said, "I guess my parents did."

He asked, "Does that work for you?"

I said, "Yes."

"Even though you don't understand it, you just flip the switch and the lights come on?"

I said, "Yep, works every time."

He said, "The system is like electricity. Every one who has ever followed it precisely, and who has been willing to change and get better themselves and not quit, has created a six-figure income; everyone who has tried to shortcut it, or to succeed without it, has failed. You don't have to understand all the psychology behind it, in fact, I don't know if anyone does completely, all we know is that it works. So all you have to do is to FLIP THE SWITCH. Listen to a business recording every day, read a minimum of fifteen minutes a day from a recommended book, get on the voicemail system, go to the seminars and conventions to associate with, and learn from successful people, counsel with your mentor regularly, follow the pattern, do the work, and don't quit, and you'll create a six figure income, and then someone will put you on a stage and want you to teach them how to succeed in business. If you don't understand it, don't sit in the dark and stay broke. Just **FLIP THE SWITCH!**"

One thing I found out later was that all of those training materials and meetings were tax deductible, and that by taking all of the tax deductions I could legally take for owning a business, I was actually able to lower my taxes that were due and get a refund from what had been taken out of my paycheck. The refund was enough to pay for all of the meetings and training materials I had purchased that year. Check with your accountant to find out what you can legitimately deduct as a business owner.

On the way home I decided to just treat the business like electricity and if it worked like he said it would, I would be a regular customer at fancy eating places like the Vanderbilt Plaza. When I walked in, the maitre de (the guy who greets you with a foreign accent) would greet us, "Good evening Mr. & Mrs.

Hendricks, how wonderful to see you this evening, would you like your usual table?" Imagine how that would make you feel compared to pulling through a drive through and hearing the speaker blare out, "Welcome to ..... can I take your order?"

Son Kevin, daughter Susan, Betty and Ralph
with Crystal Gayle (center)

Ralph & Betty with Legendary Football Coach Lou Holtz

Ralph & Betty with Pat Riley,
President and Head Coach of the Miami Heat

⌒ · CHAPTER · ⌒

TEN

It had been over a month since I had gotten together with my mentor because I had become angry over something that he had said. Some of my business partners had done something unusual and it had gotten them excited enough to start moving forward with their business. When I learned about it the next week and mentioned it to Ralph, he had told me straight out, no fluff, that what they had decided to do was a bad move and that I needed to put a stop to it. He tried to explain to me why it was a bad move, but I honestly couldn't see that he was right, because it seemed to me that if I put a stop to what they were doing, it would put a complete stop to their involvement in the business and hurt their financial future, and I felt like that was not the right thing to do from a moral perspective. It had even gotten into a heated, high volume discussion. He said that if I wouldn't change it, then he would have to be opposed to my decision, because he was going to be loyal to his current mentor. It sounded as if he was saying that I was not being loyal to him. I never thought of being disloyal to him, I just couldn't see that what he expected me to do was the right moral thing to do. I was so mad that I left and made the decision to let things go the way they were going.

As it turned out, in the long run, he was right. It was a bad business decision on my part. I learned several things from that incident. When someone is speaking from experience, they probably know what is right or wrong better than someone with no experience. When you are in the middle of the jungle, the path that appears to be the right way to go, could lead to disaster. If there is someone on a higher level that has a broader view, listen to him or her.

I also learned that even though my mentor was now a close friend, he wouldn't be disloyal to his mentors to keep my friendship. I later learned that even though I had made a bad mistake, and had gone against his advice, he was still willing to be my coach when I got over being mad and came back around.

Thank goodness I was an independent business owner, and he couldn't fire me. Every time my business growth slowed down I made it a point to get back together with Ralph. Sometimes he would answer my questions; sometimes he wouldn't even address them, but would take me out looking at things I couldn't afford. After meeting with him my business would always move forward again, so I finally figured out that if the desire is strong enough, your circumstances become irrelevant. I still might not know the answer I came looking for, but I left with a burning desire to have something I had never really considered before, so my activity level would skyrocket and my business would grow faster.

Finally I had come for some advice and we ended up at the BMW dealership. This man looked at cars, houses, jewelry, boats, motorcycles, and motor coaches more than anybody I had ever known. We test-drove a special edition 800 series that had an all leather interior. Leather seats, dash, door panels, headliner, and steering wheel; leather everywhere. Even though it was a big car, weighing over four thousand pounds, it was very fast, very smooth, and very quiet. I could take up three pages talking about it, but I'll just suggest that you go try one out sometime, even if you can't afford it right now.

There was a convention coming up that I was planning on attending. When I asked if he would be there, he said, "I'll be there with bells on." I remembered seeing a long weathered leather strip with bells on it hanging from one of the doors at his house. I said, "I've heard you say that before, what does that mean, 'with bells on'?"

He said, "In the early days of this country during the winter when there was snow on the ground, the only way to get around conveniently was in a horse or mule drawn sleigh. Because of the narrow streets and paths and blind corners, it was hard to tell if anyone was coming since there were no traffic signals. People often got run over when they came around a corner. So they put together bells on long strips of leather and laid those across the neck or shoulders of their horse. So with every step, the sleigh bells, as they were called, would jingle, and let people know that there was a sleigh coming. Sometimes a sleigh would slide off the road and get stuck so bad that the lone animal could not pull it out. So when another sleigh came along that was willing to help pull you out, if you offered to pay him and he refused, it became a common practice to give that person your sleigh bells to put on his horse, as an indication that he had helped someone out with no thought of reward."

"Of course there were some people who would go about their business but never bother to take the time to help someone else out. Then there were those people who were willing to help out anyone they came across, regardless of their own busy time schedule, regardless of the other person's race, religion, social status, politics, or whatever. Those people ended up with rows and rows of sleigh bells draped across their animals."

"In those days, a man's word was his bond. When he told someone that he would be there, it meant just that. He would be there and you could count on it. In today's society, if someone says that they will be there, it generally means that they will be there if they remember, if nothing more important comes up, if there is nothing good on television, and if their spouse says that it is okay for them to come."

"The majority of people today will never succeed at anything simply because they can't make a commitment and stand behind it. Most people's commitment only lasts as long as it is convenient. When the going gets rougher than they expected, their commitment goes out the window."

"The phrase, 'I'll be there with bells on', means I absolutely will be there, you can count on it, and not only that, but I will have helped some other people out along the way. Meaning that I am not going to be selfish and self centered, looking out only for myself."

"In our business, when you show up with bells on, not only will you get what you want financially, but you will have the love, respect, and appreciation of a lot of people that you have helped along the way."

I said, "Sounds like the story of the good Samaritan."

He said, "There are a lot of things you can learn from that story. One thing that most people miss is the fact that the man carried enough cash to help someone else. They didn't have checks or credit cards back then, so he had the cash on him to take the stranger to the emergency room, pay for his treatment, then take him to a hotel and pay for his room and meals for a week in advance, and then tell the hotel keeper that if the man spent more than that, he would pay him the additional expense when he came back through. If the Lord intended for us to be like the good Samaritan, then we need to learn to produce enough income not only to take care of our own family, but enough to be able to help other people in need."

I said, "That's a good point, I've never thought of that. I only thought about the fact that we should have the *willingness* to help others. I guess that having a good helpful attitude probably wouldn't go far with a hospital, a hotel, or a restaurant. They usually want cash."

Ralph said, "A lot of people think that a crises will develop character in a person and it may, but what a crises really does, is to reveal the true character a person already has. People can put on a good show when everything is going their way, but when a crises, or an opportunity comes along, the type of person that they really are deep down usually comes out. The priest, in the story, may have been highly thought of in the community as a kind, loving, helpful type person. But when the opportunity came along to prove all of that to the world, it actually revealed that he was a selfish, self-centered person who wasn't concerned with his fellow man. The Bible clearly teaches that the freedom of choice will reveal the true character of a man. Like the story of the prodigal son, who had been a 'good little boy' until his father gave him his inheritance. Then he went off living a riotous life. The money didn't cause him to go bad, it just gave him the financial ability to go and do what he wanted to do all along, but couldn't afford to."

I said, "So money can also reveal the true character of a person."

"That's right. Good people will do good things when they get a lot of money, evil-minded people will do evil things. Anyone that says that money will cause people to go bad, is probably thinking of all the evil things that they would do, if they came into a lot of money."

I said, "So a crises is actually an opportunity to let the world see what kind of person you really are, and earning a lot of money just releases you to do whatever you have always dreamed of doing, whether good or bad. I guess I have an opportunity right now because our business has suffered some serious setbacks lately."

Ralph said, "You only find out if you are a champion after you get knocked down, not when you are winning and everything is going your way. After you get knocked down we find out what you are really made of."

I was glad that we had that discussion. I had grown up with the impression that rich people go to hell. So I had never wanted to get rich, I just wanted to get right up to the edge of it, without going over the line. Once I studied the Bible and saw that many of the heroes of the Bible were rich people, it became obvious that God doesn't care if you are rich or poor, he looks at your heart, and your attitude. And since that was the case, as long as I was doing a lot of good with my time and my money, and keeping Him first in my life, the good Lord probably wouldn't mind if I cruised down the road doing my good deeds in a flashy new BMW. Man, was that thing awesome!

CHAPTER

E L E V E N

I had mentioned one time that I loved to go out target shooting and that I liked guns, and he must have made a mental note of it. I knew that he wasn't into guns that much, but here we were going from one gun shop to the next. I could have spent a fortune, if I had had one to spend. The subject of what you sow, you reap, came up.

He said, "There are a lot of lessons that can be learned from the parable of the sower, but most people never learn to apply them to their daily lives. The most obvious lesson is that what you sow in the earth, you reap. The principle also holds true outside the plant world. If you sow hatred into a child, you will reap an adult that spews hatred. If you raise a child with love, you end up with a loving adult. If while you are raising a child, you tell him repeatedly that he is no good and that he will end up in jail, that is exactly where he will end up, not because he was bad, but because you programmed him to end up there. A friend of mine used to go into prisons and speak, and on one occasion he was talking about how children are raised. On a whim, he decided to ask a question. He asked, 'How many of you were told as you were growing up, that you were bad, and that you would end up in prison? If you would, stand up.' There were several hundred inmates there, and every single one of them stood up. My friend got so emotional that he couldn't even go on with his talk. He wondered how many of these people could have lived a happy and productive life, if their parents had just loved them, encouraged them, and told them that they would rise above all their challenges, to become good citizens."

Thinking back, I remembered all the times that my mom and dad had encouraged me, "You can do better than that. You're smart; you can make good grades. You know that you shouldn't be doing those kinds of things; you've just been hanging around with the wrong crowd. You can do anything that you set your mind to. You may go through some hard times, but just keep your moral standards high and you'll be alright."

Ralph said, "The principle holds true in the financial world. If you want a harvest of more money and more free time, then you have to sow, or invest some of your money or your free time into something that can give you back more time and money later."

"Another lesson is that you will reap in proportion to what you sow. Plant one corn seed and get one corn stalk. If you plant ten, you get ten stalks. Plant ten thousand, and you get back ten thousand stalks. So the more you plant, the more you will harvest."

"Then there is the lesson of multiplication. When you plant one corn kernel, you don't get back one kernel, you get a stalk with several ears of corn, each containing hundreds of kernels. So one corn seed can feed any number of people from now on."

"Of course, it will only do that if you take into consideration the lesson of delayed gratification. If you eat the corn seed now, you get one swallow, and you will still be hungry. If you plant it, or invest it, and then watch and protect your investment, then it produces one stalk, several ears, and hundreds or thousands of seeds which can be replanted, reinvested, to produce thousands of stalks, tens of thousands of ears, which will give you back enough to feed thousands of people, as well as enough to replant and feed thousands of people from now on."

"In reality there is no shortage of raw material in the world, there is only a shortage of ideas, or of knowledge and understanding."

I said, "What do you mean a shortage of knowledge and understanding."

He said, "Years ago there was a severe food shortage in a small country. As usual the United States was the first country to respond to the need. We sent cargo ships over with enough food to last several months, and enough seed of different types, to literally cover their country with food to feed them from now on. Within six months there was another call for help. When our people went back, they found the country still barren, and the people once again starving. They had not only eaten the food, but instead of planting, they had also eaten the seed. There was not a shortage of food in this country; there was a lack of understanding of the principles of delayed gratification and multiplication. The sad part is, you see the same pattern going on, every day, all around us, on a smaller scale. People earn more money than it takes to live, and then they spend every dime of it, instead of investing some of it into their future. There is literally enough food that falls to the ground every year and doesn't get harvested, to feed the world. There are enough trees in one forest in Germany to build a house for everyone on earth. There is enough income coming into many families to live comfortably until they die, but they don't invest any of their income, they just spend it all. There is no shortage of raw material; there is just a shortage of knowledge."

I asked, "So why am I always hearing about a shortage of this or that, for example, oil?"

He said, "Because the perception of a shortage drives the prices up and makes billions of dollars of profit for the companies who market those products. Typically, if a company or an industry has been paying millions of dollars to advertise in the media and that industry sends out a press release about a shortage, the media will run the story. They don't have the capability to do an in-depth study to find out the exact facts; they just report it as news. The shortage may be real, or it may be exaggerated. There is natural supply and demand, and then there is artificially created shortages to increase demand, and raise prices."

I said, "I've noticed that every time the weather man predicts snow, every grocery store in town sells out and has empty shelves. Many times it doesn't snow when they predict it. I've always wondered if the grocery stores were in cahoots with the weather man."

He laughed, and said, "Well, I don't know about that, but there is a direct correlation between the amount of money a company spends on advertising, and the image of that company that is presented to the public by the media. If you don't spend any money on advertising, don't expect to hear your name, or your company mentioned by the media. If they do mention you, it may be in a very negative light. Too many people think that 'news' programs are there to report exactly what happened in our world but that isn't necessarily so. They are there just like every other program. Programs are put on the air because someone is willing to pay for advertising during that broadcast. If a program attracts a lot of viewers or listeners, the network can sell advertising and make the company money. So what matters to them is to increase audience share to be able to sell the products or services of the people who are paying to advertise on that show. The reporter on the street may, or may not be biased, but by the time the story gets on the air it may be twisted to make it more interesting, or controversial, or it may be sensationalized, or have relevant facts omitted to increase the audience and improve ratings. Sometimes the system will reward people for digging up dirt to improve ratings, at the expense of the truth, more than it rewards them for just reporting the facts. They may or may not be deliberately trying to manipulate your way of thinking, but the goal of improved ratings and more profit creates the same end result. You scratch my back and I'll scratch yours. It goes on every day all over the world."

I said, "You scratch my back, I'll scratch yours, sounds like most of the politicians I know."

He said, "Well, that is often very true in politics. How a representative votes on any issue, many times, is in direct proportion to how much money has been donated to him, or her, or their campaign, by a particular company or industry. That's why the lobbyists are so powerful. They spend millions of dollars to get laws passed that make their companies billions."

"So, back to sowing and reaping," I said. You reap what you sow. You reap in proportion to how much you sow. You get back much more than you sow. You don't get it back immediately, it comes back later on."

"Right," he said. "Then there is the lesson that is explained in the Bible, that some seed falls on shallow ground and dies, some gets choked out by weeds, some produces thirty times what you planted, some sixty times, and some a hundred times what you planted. Your job is just to go out and plant lots of seeds, whatever that may be in your business, and the results will come."

I said, "So planting seeds would be like advertising, or doing presentations in our business?"

He said, "Sure, if you compare advertising for your business to sowing seeds, some advertising gets zero response, some creates a sprout of interest that doesn't go anywhere, some gets good results, some better, and some advertising gets phenomenal results. The small part that gets a hundred to one results makes it worth all the time, effort, and money that was spent on the seed that got little or no results."

As I was digesting that concept, Ralph said, "The challenge in our business, is that we have no way of knowing which person we talk to is going to be the one that brings us phenomenal results and helps us to secure our financial future. So you have to approach every person, or prospect, as if they are the one."

Then Ralph said something that was very discouraging and totally blew my mind.

"About ninety five percent of all the time and effort you put into this business will be totally wasted, and won't produce any benefit, long term."

I was devastated. Ninety five percent of all my effort, year after year was wasted? How could I go on, knowing that? Why go out and do anything at all?

As I was sitting there in stunned silence, he said, "The other five percent of your effort will make you rich beyond your wildest dreams. You won't ever have to work for another man as long as you live, unless you choose to. You can live in a mansion anywhere you choose, anywhere in the world. You can drive whatever vehicle you want, and the price won't even be a factor in your decision. You'll be free to live life on your terms."

It is truly amazing how a person's attitude can go from the bottom of the barrel to the top of the world in five seconds. I said, "Well let me ask you this, is there any way I can skip that ninety five percent part and just do the five percent?"

As he was laughing, he said, "To my knowledge no one has ever figured that out. But it is still worth it in the long run. You just have to be willing to do enough work, and pay enough of a price to make sure that you get the five percent done, and stay around long enough to see the end result of all your efforts. Too many people get involved and put forth a lot of effort and spend a lot of time working at it, but then they quit. They'll never know if they just didn't get to the five percent, or if they had found them and planted the seed, but quit and left before the harvest came in from their effort."

I saw my business in a whole new light. "So the sooner I get through all that other ninety five percent crap, the sooner I get to the five percent, and the lifestyle?"

"Exactly."

On the way home I was visualizing a huge concrete room in my basement, with a door like a bank vault, to hold row after row of firearms and ammunition. My own shooting range underground, where I could shoot any time of day or night without bothering the neighbors. Never mind the neighbors, I would own so much land, that they couldn't hear me shoot anyway. I couldn't wait to get started working my way through that ninety five percent to get to the five percent that would start the multiplication process and make me wealthy.

Ralph & Betty with Dave Thomas,
Founder of Wendy's Restaurants

⌐～⚬ · CHAPTER · ⚬～⌐

TWELVE

I came across some statistics in an article that got me worried about whether our industry would last. So as usual, I called my mentor and set up a time to get together. We were going through the Parade of Homes looking at homes that cost several million dollars.

I said, "A guy I that I work with brought some information to my attention that I wasn't aware of before." I then told him about the information which seemed to be negative about our business.

He said, "A dog in the hunt doesn't know it has fleas."

I turned and looked at him, wondering what earthly connection negative statistics could possibly have to do with bird hunting.

He said, "Your dad had bird dogs as you were growing up didn't he?"

"Yes."

"What were they doing most of the time that they spent in your back yard while they were not hunting?"

"Well, I think mostly sleeping, eating, and scratching at fleas."

"Okay, now think back to the times you were out hunting. Did you ever see a dog that was on a scent, stop and scratch?"

"No."

He said, "The same is true in this business. The people who are out building it fast and furious are not even consciously aware of the people out there who have negative opinions of what we do. If you are sitting at home doing nothing, then you become more aware of those little nips and bites of ridicule and criticism, and you start to pay attention to them. But a dog in the hunt doesn't even know it has fleas, much less, stop and pay attention to them, he's too busy accomplishing what he came to do. There are people who are negative about every business, every profession and every idea in the world, and they are usually very vocal about their opinions. Negative people or negative opinions can't stop you from building a big business and becoming wealthy unless you stop being active, and start spending all your time analyzing the opinions of others who have never accomplished anything."

I said, "That makes sense, but what about these statistics, doesn't that prove what they are saying?"

He said, "You can prove anything you want to with statistics. Statistics are often times used by people who don't have facts, or proof, to back up what they have chosen to believe. Statistics are just numbers, which may leave out some relevant information, which changes your perception. For example, years ago when Harvard was an all men's school, and Vassar was an all women's school, they did a study which showed that the average Harvard graduate in their lifetime, had 2.6 children, while the average Vassar graduate in their lifetime had 2.3 children. So the statistics seem to prove that men have more children than women do. Would you believe that, just because that is what the statistics prove?"

I said, "Men don't have babies, women have all of them."

"Exactly. But that is one vital tidbit of information that doesn't show up in the statistics, and if a person did not already know that, then he could be led to believe, by statistics, that something is true, which is totally false and ridiculous. So whenever you are looking at statistics, be sure and get all of the relevant information regarding the subject. You only get relevant information from people who are involved. Taking advice from anyone about any subject that they are not involved with, and very knowledgeable about, would be insane."

I said, "I guess that's true, some people think that all attorneys are shysters, all doctors are incompetent quacks, and all accountants cook the books to cover the truth, and they believe that way because they knew one person who really was like that, or because they heard of one who was like that. So they project the bad image onto everyone in that business, career or profession."

Ralph said, "The truth of the matter is that there are good people in every profession and there are also incompetent and some-times evil people in every profession. If someone has been lied to or taken advantage of by someone in a particular field, they generally view everyone in that field with suspicion. It is up to each individual to decide how they are going to live and how they are going to run their business or profession. If you run into someone who was taken advantage of in the past, and has a bad attitude about all business owners as a result, don't let that affect your attitude towards our entire industry. You just do what is right, and run your business with honesty and integrity."

I couldn't believe that people actually lived in houses like the ones we were walking through, but I guess they did. There were neighborhoods all around Nashville with homes like these.

I said, "I've been talking to a lot of people who seem to think that they have it made because they have a high paying job, or they are already self employed and stay very busy. They say that with the amount of time I'm putting into the business, I could be making a lot more money doing some other things."

He said, "That's probably true in the short term. But, whatever you do, you need to be in business for yourself. You need to own it, control it, so that you can earn the profit from your efforts. As long as you work for another man, or a company, you will have a ceiling on your income and you will never get paid what you are worth. Essentially, they are buying your life for wholesale, selling it at retail, and keeping the profit. You need to put yourself into a position to earn the profit from your own effort, as well as earning from the effort of others. When he was the richest man on earth, J. Paul Getty said that he would rather earn one percent each from the efforts of one hundred men, than to earn one hundred percent from his own effort."

I nodded, "That makes sense. You could make as much money, or more, without even doing any of the work."

"If you are going to enjoy the fruits of Free Enterprise and Capitalism," he said, "you have to own the enterprise. It has to be yours. If you don't own it, you are probably working for a corporation that doesn't have a heart. It doesn't care about your children. It makes decisions based on the bottom line. Which is not evil. That's just a fact of life. To enjoy the fruits of freedom, you have to set a goal to own something, nurture it, pour yourself into it, be really good to it for a while, so that it will be good to you from then on. We all get paid in direct proportion to the amount of service that we have given to others outside of our families. Look at what you are doing for others today, outside of what you have to do, and you can predict your future lifestyle."

I said, "Based on my lifestyle today, I guess I haven't really been of much service to very many other people."

Ralph said, "Instead of taking the advice of broke people and going out and getting another job, picture yourself where you want to be and start moving forward. If that way fails, another door will always open. When you make a decision and get committed, even if you don't know how you are going to do it, things start to happen that you hadn't planned on. Doors begin to open that weren't there before. So just set the goal and begin moving toward it, even if you can't clearly see how you can accomplish it. Every noble goal, at first, seems unattainable. Begin to work toward your dream and the picture will come into focus. Start to participate in your dream. Not as soon as you believe it, or as soon as your circumstances change, start now to participate in it."

As I was going through the million-dollar mansion I was thinking about participating in my dream. How do you do that? I came to the entertainment room with the big screen HDTV, surround sound, and six overstuffed chairs. The movie *'Top Gun'* was playing so I decided to sit down for just a second. I could feel and hear those jets screaming all the way around me. I was screaming through the clear blue sky at mach two, upside down shooting down the bad guys. Twenty minutes later someone tapped me on the shoulder and brought me back to earth. I had almost forgotten where I was. Perhaps that was what he meant by 'start participating in your dream'. Now I knew that a big screen entertainment room would be in one room of my dream home, which twenty minutes before, I had never thought about before.

As we went through the next home I went back to the conversation about negativity. I mentioned that one of my business partners had come across a website on the Internet that was negative about our business.

He said, "First of all, you need to realize that at this time there are absolutely no laws about what you can or can't put on the Internet. If they put that stuff in magazines or newspapers they would be found guilty of liable, slander, defamation, and other charges because they can be proven false. But on the world-wide-web they don't have to document what they claim at all. They don't even have to show who is putting the false information out there. So anyone who gets offended by a person in this industry can go online and slam the entire business with no repercussions. So basically you can get the same quality of information from the Internet as you get from the papers you see at grocery store checkout lanes and from bathroom walls. If you believe that Elvis is still alive, and that little green Martians visit us regularly, go ahead and believe what you read on negative Internet web sites. People with credible information will tell you who the author is that is putting the information out and they will document their sources and their claims. If they don't, it is probably just opinion or totally fictitious. The most effective negative websites will put a lot of provable truth on their site and claim to be unbiased, and then slip in the lies and slander with the truth. Because there is so much truth, many people will be sucked into believing the lies that are there. Many times negative web sites are put out by losers who didn't have what it takes to succeed, who are trying to justify their failure. Once you explain these things to people they should be able to move on. If they don't, its just because they don't want to be involved in the business for a personal reason. And once that decision is made, one excuse is as good as another."

I determined that a home on a golf course would be great. No matter what time of year that you looked out the window you would always have a beautiful view of manicured grounds. There would be no nosey neighbors directly behind you, watching everything you did. Even if you didn't play golf, this would be a nice place to live.

 ~ · CHAPTER · ~

THIRTEEN

Business was finally going better for my wife and myself. We had qualified for a trip to Hawaii with our mentors. Now it was Tuesday, and we were sunning ourselves on the beach of the biggest island, called Hawaii Island. It was late morning, about seventy six degrees, the sky was clear, with a five mile an hour trade wind very gently flowing by. The beach was practically deserted as far as you could see. This Island was more secluded than Honolulu, where you couldn't even find a place to lay a beach towel on the sand because of the thousands of tourists basting in the sun.

In our conversation I mentioned that even though I had gotten to a point that I could quit my job and focus more time on my business, I still didn't seem to be able to have the lifestyle that I wanted. I told him that we were making more money than we ever had, but we were still basically living month to month and spending all the money that we made.

He looked over and said, "That's because you've probably never been taught the principle of the four buckets."

Knowing that I was ignorant of this subject, because I had never heard of a principle involving four buckets before, I said, "Okay, so tell me about the four buckets."

He leveled out a spot, and drew four bucket shapes in the sand. Then he put a number in each bucket, one through four. "Do you have enough money coming in to cover your current expenses; house, car payments, utilities, and stuff like that?"

"Yes."

"Okay, this is what you should do with any money you get that is over and above your bare necessities.

You don't want to lose your home, so take care of that, and then put your money into these four buckets. The first bucket that you want to put money into is your business. Make sure that you keep enough money going back into the business that it can continue to operate efficiently. Buy whatever materials, tools, and supplies you need to keep the business in a growing and expanding mode. Don't overspend to the point that you have things lying around not being utilized, but make sure that you do have what you need based on how fast you are growing. We've talked about this before. Remember, to enjoy the fruits of Capitalism and Free Enterprise you have to own the enterprise. Take care of your enterprise first, and then it will take care of you for the rest of your life."

"That's not what most of the financial wizards teach." I said, "Most of them teach people to start out by paying off all of their debts."

"It's Tuesday, late morning, and you are lying on the beach in Hawaii with no job to go home to. Where would you be right now if you had put all of your focus for the last two years on getting out of debt, instead of focusing on building a successful business enterprise?"

I smiled, "I'd still be working at the factory, or something similar, and I doubt that I could ever have earned enough money on my job to get out of debt without giving up the apartment and living in the back of my pickup truck."

Ralph smiled, "There is nothing wrong with teaching people how to get out of debt and the people who do that are providing a great service to people. Most debt reduction experts teach systems that will work, if you stick with them. So if a person's primary goal is to get out of debt and eliminate that stress from their lives, then that is the pattern they should follow. However, if you want to become wealthy you need to start with bucket number one. Create a business entity that you can develop to a point where it will pay you a residual income whether you continue to work or not. Build it to a point that it will pay you many times more than you could ever have made swapping hours for dollars. Which means that you have to build a business where you can duplicate your efforts through others so that your entire income is not dependent on the number of hours that you can work. Then you can pay off all the debts very quickly and easily."

He said, "I heard a statement one time that if you serve the 'classes', you live with the 'masses', but if you serve the 'masses', you live with the 'classes'." Most people work a job and serve the 'classes', which is the wealthy people who own the company, so they live with the 'masses'. If you want to live with the 'classes', start a business whereby you can serve the 'masses'."

He went on, "The debt reduction experts are basically providing a service to people who are in debt, which is about ninety-five percent of the population, or the 'masses'. By doing that, they are getting very, very rich, because they are doing what I just explained to you. They are building a business that serves thousands of people, and they can duplicate themselves all over the country through books, audio recordings, videos, television shows, radio shows, etc. They may have gotten out of debt using their system, but they get rich with bucket number one, by building a business. So if you want to get out of debt, do what they say. If you want to get rich, do what they do."

He pointed to the second bucket, "Once you have funded the business, begin to put any additional money you have into bucket number two. Which is paying off all of your debts. There are several good books on that subject which will teach you very effective methods of accomplishing that and I highly recommend them."

Pointing to the third sand pail he said, "After you have paid off all of your debts, begin to put money into bucket number three; investments. I'm not talking about gambling. A lot of people take their hard earned money and put it into the stock market, mutual funds, etc. and think that they are investing. They are *hoping* that their 'investment' will go up in value, but they don't have any clue whether it will go up or down in value. In my opinion they are not investing they are gambling. Unfortunately, the vast majority of them will lose all, or most of their money over a long period of time. If you don't know that you are going to make money going into a deal, with a very high degree of certainty, then you are gambling. Before making any investments, find a mentor who is a professional investor to learn from. You should be very careful of taking investing advice from someone who is in a position to make money from your investment whether you make money or not. You should never take investment advice from a friend, a relative, or a co-worker with a 'hot tip', unless they are wealthy professional investors themselves."

He continued, "When you have enough investments in place that you can continue to live your current lifestyle from the income from your investments, then put your money into bucket number four, lifestyle."

"That's when you go out and pay cash for a vehicle, take trips to exotic locations, buy your wife all the diamonds, jewelry, and designer clothing she wants, have interior decorators furnish your home with expensive stuff to impress other people, and whatever else you want to do. If you have taken care of the first three buckets before you start paying for lifestyle, you won't have to worry about making payments because you'll pay cash."

"You won't have to worry about having things repossessed, and you won't have to be stressed because you can't pay your bills. Everything will be taken care of before you start buying the trinkets."

"Wow." I said, "That is just the opposite of the way most people live their lives. Most folks work a job, earn money, and then go out and finance as much lifestyle as the creditors will allow."

He nodded, "Which puts them into debt for the rest of their lives. It creates stress and problems, which get worse and worse because of the effects of compound interest. They can never quit working because if they do, they lose their house, their car, the big screen television, the furniture, and everything else they had financed. They never have any source of residual income, never get debt free, and never have enough investments to come anywhere near supporting them. They spent all of their hard earned money trying to finance enough stuff to *appear* to have a good lifestyle." He said, "I saw a survey years ago that stated that most people's goal in life is to 'appear to other people to be doing well'. If that is your goal, you will spend all of your money on down payments for things that you can't afford to buy, so that you will look good to others. Which guarantees that you will never be 'doing well', because you never fill the buckets in the right order to become wealthy."

As I rolled over to get some sun on my back I remembered some friends of mine that had gone through a debt reduction program and as soon as they had all of their consumer debt paid off they went out and financed a new car because 'they could now afford the payment'. I don't think that is what the financial advisors teach.

I asked, "So if getting wealthy is that simple, why don't more people get wealthy?"

He sat back in his chair and looked up at the beautiful blue sky and at the surf rolling in, and finally said, "There are probably a lot of reasons, but the biggest reason that the vast majority of people won't become wealthy is because they never have a bucket number one. Most people never even attempt to start a business of their own.

Roughly ninety five percent of those who do start one will go out of business within the first five to ten years, for different reasons. Most enterprises are not capable of creating a residual income because of the way they are structured. They are really a way to own your own job. When you, as the business owner, stop working, the money stops coming in. Many people who get involved in a business like ours, that does have the potential to create walk away income, simply don't have the discipline to stick with it long term, until it pays off. The learning curve to become an effective business owner is between two and five years for most people, and the majority of people won't stay involved in the education and training program that long without seeing substantial profit. They have employee mentality. They expect to get paid immediately for the work they have done this week, or this month, or even in the first couple years. But a successful business that will pay a substantial residual income will take longer than that. Many are unwilling to take advice from those who have succeeded before them. They grew up with the movie images of the lone hero that takes on the world by himself and wins, and they think they can do that in business."

I said, "I resemble that remark."

He chuckled, "Well, your lone wolf approach only cost you about two years before you figured out that you couldn't do it alone. Many people never figure it out. They go down the tubes without ever getting humble and asking someone else for help. Then they blame their failure on the business opportunity. True wealth can only be created by putting together a team of people who work together for the mutual benefit of everyone involved."

I personally knew quite a few people that had fallen into the category of failing and then blaming everyone around them for their failure.

He said, "Others get distracted by the daily cares and activities of life and just don't give the business the attention it needs to succeed. Some are unwilling to change personally and grow into the kind of person that others would want to be associated with. People who don't succeed in a big way are not losers they are just average people."

As I looked out across the crystal clear water and the turquoise colored waves rolling to the horizon and breathed in the fresh clean air I thought to myself, "if people don't succeed so that they can have the freedom to travel, wake up when they choose, not have a boss, and have all the trinkets, then they have definitely lost out. They may not be losers, but they definitely lose."

I realized that I had not had any hay fever or allergies since I had arrived. "I wonder how come the air is so clean and fresh in Hawaii?"

"Possibly because it had to travel over thousands of miles of ocean and it has been rained on hundreds of times which would have washed all the pollution and impurities out before it got here."

Scientifically I didn't know if that was accurate, but it sounded good to me.

I said, "So how do you convince your spouse to use the four bucket principle, when she wants a nicer house, a newer car, better furniture, flashier jewelry, and new clothes right now? By the way, did you know that my wife is an angel? She is always up in the air about something, she never has an earthly thing to wear, and she always seems to be harping on something."

He laughed and said, "Well, if you will take the time to explain what you are doing and why, and show her how the four buckets will benefit her in the long run, she'll probably go along with you without too much of a fuss. Assuming of course that you are out putting the business together and she can see things progressing. Then, if you will become the man that she thought that she married, and fill those four buckets up, all that harping noise will go away."

Ralph always put the responsibility for my success or failure squarely in my lap, whether I wanted it there or not.

"Actually, my wife has handled delayed gratification extremely well," I said. "In fact, our first Christmas after we started our business when money was extremely tight, I had the choice of buying her a present, or buying some advertising materials, which we really needed at the time, to help our business expand, so I bought her a Christmas card, and a whole case of advertising tapes. She was okay with it because she understood, but her family and friends thought I was a real ....whatever. Our second Christmas we had more money than the year before, but the business was growing too, so that year I bought her two cases of advertising tapes. I really caught a lot of flak for that. So I actually did take care of bucket number one first, because that's what you taught me to do, but then after that, I've been putting money into number four, instead of knocking out all the debt and investing."

He nodded, "Usually if a man is stretching himself to do what it takes to be successful his wife won't complain, even if it is taking longer than she would like. But when they both know what has to be done and he's laying on the couch, or afraid to get outside of his comfort zone and do something new, then she gets irritated, because she believes in him, and he's not living up to her image of him as a man. To be successful in any arena you have to be pushing the envelope."

"What does that mean?"

"It's a term we used in the Air Force. We knew that the jets we were flying were safe up to a certain altitude, so as long as we stayed below that point we were in a comfort zone, or a safe zone. Sometimes the turbulence or other factors would force you out of the comfort zone so that you were pushing the envelope of the aircrafts capability. Sometimes you did it just for the thrill. You've never been more alive than when you were way out there on the edge, in the danger zone."

At this point Ralph was sitting up on the edge of his beach chair, his eyes sparkling, talking fast and very animated.

"There were a few of the guys that lived for that rush that you got and they were always pushing the envelope further and further, testing themselves and their aircraft to see what they were capable of. Someone said that you have never really lived, until you've almost died, and these guys wanted to live life to the max, so they would push it until they were staring death right in the face..."

His voice trailed off and he sat back, as he stared up into the stratosphere, reliving a memory. He reminded me off an eagle, created to soar through the heavens and reign supreme, sitting on a perch, staring off into space.

After a minute I said, "I don't suppose that one of those guys was named Ralph Autry?"

He came back down to earth, looked at me and smiled real big, "My superior officers would get so ticked off when they got wind of how high we'd gone, or when someone would report a jet flying upside down a hundred feet off the deck."

Then his tone got serious. "If you want to be successful in anything Mister, you have to be willing to get outside of your comfort zone, to push the limits of your capabilities, to attempt to do things you've never done before. You may not get the physical rush that a jet pilot does, but when you are out there in *your* danger zone, doing things you've never done before, going places you've never been before, you will feel more alive than ever. You'll feel your heart thumping and feel the blood rushing through your veins. You'll never know how high you can go in a jet or in business until you've stood it on its tail and kicked in the afterburners. So when you realize that something needs to be done to move your business forward, and it's outside your envelope, take a deep breath, shove the throttle to the firewall, and let out a rebel yell as you do it. After you have done it once, the new activity becomes part of your comfort zone."

Later, as I was snorkeling around the coral reefs observing the thousands of brightly colored fish darting in and out, I remembered a statistic I had come across. Only two percent of the population of the United States ever gets to visit Hawaii. Of those two percent who do get to visit, only two percent of those ever get to come back for a second visit. The place really is like paradise. I was glad that I had finally created a business that paid my family a residual income so that I had the freedom to come and enjoy it. The fact that I didn't have a job waiting for me when I got home was even better. I was glad that I had been willing to stick with it, and grow, and learn, and push myself outside of my comfort zone, because the rewards were definitely worth not being average.

Since that first trip, we have been back to Hawaii two more times, to Oahu and Kauai, and will go many more times. We also took a weeklong cruise up the Inside Passage of Alaska on one of the nicest cruise ships in the world. We enjoyed it so much that my wife and I did it again a few years later and paid for both our parents to go with us. That didn't repay them for all the things they have done for us in our lives, but they all really enjoyed it. We spent a week in Atlantis Resort on Paradise Island, Bahamas, and have been to a lot of other places that 'average' people seldom get to experience.

When I got back to the room after snorkeling and successfully avoiding 'Jaws', I got a note pad out and made a note of the four buckets to put my money into.

Bucket 1: Business.

Bucket 2: Pay off debts.

Bucket 3: Investments.

Bucket 4: Lifestyle.

After reading the biographies of many very successful people, I find that most, if not all of them followed this pattern. Sam Walton continued to drive an old pick up truck until he was a multi-millionaire. His desk was made of two sawhorses and a door laid across them. He put his money into his business first, and lifestyle last, and became the richest man in America at one point in time.

I can't honestly say that we have stuck with these principles totally and absolutely, because we did indulge ourselves and purchase some nicer things along the way. But we stayed with them as close as we could, and from that point on we didn't finance stuff we couldn't afford. We just did without, or got by with what we had until we could afford to pay for what we wanted. There were times when we were putting money into bucket number three, investments, and family and friends would criticize us for the automobiles we were driving, or the fact that we didn't even have cable television. Our vehicles were paid for and they still got us where we wanted to go dependably so we were delaying the gratification of buying newer vehicles until we could either pay cash, or at least until we had invested enough of our money that the investments paid us enough cash flow to make the payments on a newer car. We won't go into my opinion about television programming. I just didn't watch it enough to make it worth the expense. The people doing the criticizing had newer vehicles and cable television, but they also had monthly payments, and they had to go to work at a job every day to make the payments because they didn't have any investments. The ninety-five percent of the people who swap hours for dollars very rarely understand the actions of the other five percent who become wealthy. Let me point out that this difference does not make them bad people; it just means that they look at money, and how to earn it differently.

Since every individual's situation is different, I strongly advise you to find a mentor who has what you want, then sit down and discuss your exact situation with them before starting any type of business, or any debt reduction strategy.

And, remember to only take advice from people who will be benefited if you succeed, and who will not make money if you fail, or lose money. If their success is tied to yours, you have a much better chance of getting good advice.

Use the four bucket principle and we may see each other on the beaches of the world!

Ralph Autry, U.S.A.F.

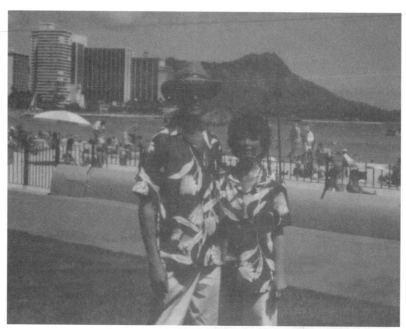

Tim & Anna on Waikiki Beach, First Hawaii trip

Ralph & Betty on stage with Tim & Anna

Tim & Anna at Mickey Mantle's Restaurant,
New York City

⌒⌒ · CHAPTER · ⌒⌒

FOURTEEN

A group of business owners had decided to take a trip to New York City just before Christmas. The city was beautiful with all the holiday decorations and lights sparkling against the night sky. We stayed at the Marriott World Trade Center and went to the top of the Towers. What an awesome view! One evening we went to see the world famous Radio City Music Hall Rockettes. Another evening we went to Broadway and saw the play 'Titanic'. We shopped at FAO Schwartz, the world's largest toy store. The food was wonderful, especially Mickey Mantle's restaurant across the street from Central Park. The city was much cleaner and safer than what I had imagined.

On this night we had all taken the Statue of Liberty dinner cruise. If you ever want to feel patriotic, take the cruise and listen to some of the stories about this wonderful country.

As we had built our business I had watched how other people reacted or responded to things that happened to them. If I saw someone react in a way that I didn't agree with, I would look at my own life to see if I did the same thing in the same type situation. One thing that I identified was that whenever something negative came up, it caused people to become inactive, including myself.

I said to Ralph, "Sometimes things will happen that make me wonder if I'm doing the right thing, and because of that doubt, the next thing I know, I've been sidetracked, and a week or two has gone by and I haven't accomplished anything."

He said, "The vast majority of people get into a situation that causes them to have doubts or misgivings and they instinctively draw back. They go inactive. Doubt causes fear and fear causes paralysis and inactivity. You'll achieve more in life than the masses by simply learning one simple principle. When in doubt, attack."

As usual he painted a word picture parable, "Imagine that you are in the military and you are a member of a six-man team that has been dropped into the jungle in the middle of the night behind enemy lines. For the next six months you eat, sleep and live twenty-four hours a day in enemy territory. You have five associates on your team. Everybody else in that jungle is an enemy who will kill you instantly if they find you. Sometimes you won't be able to see more than a few feet, but you can hear further than that. How do you survive in that situation? Number one, you do your duty, you fulfill your assignment. Every person on that team has responsibilities and if one person drops the ball, you all die. So you make sure that your job gets done, period. Number two; you do whatever it takes for the team to succeed. If someone else gets hurt or falls behind, you take up the slack. If you get the attitude that you so often hear from employees, 'That's not my job', then you are all going to die in the jungle. It's true in business too. Most employees' do the least amount that they can get by with and still keep their job and get paid. An entrepreneur does whatever it takes to reach the objective and accomplish the mission."

He continued, "But the main point is this; when you are going through the jungle and you hear something that causes doubts and fears about whether you should move on or not, you attack! You go on the offensive. Mister, if you let fear paralyze you, and you try to hide, then sooner or later the enemy will find you, and you're dead meat. When ninety five percent of the population gets scared, they pull back into a shell, like a turtle. They go inactive. They wait to see what's going to happen next. What happens is that they get crushed like a turtle in the middle of the road, or a competitor who went on the offense wipes them out."

I got a brief graphic mental image of a turtle in the road being squashed by a truck, and thought of all the people I had known who had once owned a business, but had lost it because they pulled back when they should have been hauling shell.

Ralph went on, "There will be many times in your business career when things will create doubt in your mind. The economy gets worse, or better, inflation goes up, or down, processes change, techniques change, and people come and go. The winds of social approval sometimes blow in your favor and sometimes they blow against you. Whenever you encounter a situation that causes doubt, press forward. You may not want to go charging forward with your M-16 blazing in all directions, but go on the offensive. Become the hunter, not the hunted. Don't fear the business world; make the business world fear you. When the smoke clears, you'll be ahead of ninety-five percent of the competition because they hunkered down to wait and see what was going to happen."

He said, "Don't be like the baseball player in the bottom of the ninth inning who comes to bat with the bases loaded, two outs, and his team two runs behind, and, because he fears striking out and losing the game, he lets the fear paralyze him and he never swings the bat. So he strikes out and loses the game. Don't ever do that. Develop the attitude that if I go down, I'll go down swinging. I'll fight to the last breath. If you just stand up when everyone else sits down, you'll be head and shoulders above the crowd."

He seemed to be on a roll, so I just kept listening.

"If the crap hits the fan and everyone else is peeping out of their shell or from under a rock and they see you moving forward, they will automatically attribute to you all kinds of heroic characteristics, probably out of all proportion to reality. But that is what distinguishes heroes from others that you never hear or read about. They have the ability to get themselves to take action in the face of fear, doubt, and adversity."

"Sometimes fifteen seconds of courage will identify you as a hero for the rest of your life. In the business world, fifteen seconds of overcoming your fears can change your financial future forever. One phone call, one contact, one question asked of the right person at the right time can change everything."

I remembered having fifteen seconds of courage and one phone call (to him) that had changed my life dramatically, so I had to agree with that.

He was still talking, "One thing that will help overcome doubts and fears is more information. When you have doubts, go into information gathering mode. Don't be afraid to ask questions. It is good if you can ask the right questions of the right people; but if you don't know what question to ask, then get with someone who may be in a position to know more than you, explain your doubts, and then ask them something. Getting factual information will often clear out the smoke of your doubts and fears. So never let doubt stop you. Remember, it's not what you get while you are here that counts. It's not what you accumulate that matters the most, because when you die you leave all the stuff here. What matters most is the legacy that you leave. When your flame goes out, will there still be someone here to carry the torch to light the way for others, because of your influence, and because they were inspired by your life? When you meet your maker, will he call you by name and welcome you home? Will he say, "Well done." Or will he just say, "Well?" Will he say that you fought a good fight, you finished the course, you kept the faith? Will he also welcome a lot of others home, who are there because of the influence that you had on their lives?"

Mentally reflecting on the kind of influence that I had been on other peoples lives in the past made me decide to deliberately be a better influence in the future.

Ralph finished, "Doubt cannot stop you unless you allow it to. If it doesn't kill you, then dealing with it will make you stronger. When in doubt, attack."

The cruise ship pulled up close to the statue and stopped for a while so we all went up on the top deck. It was fairly cold outside being on the water but no one seemed to mind. The view of the Statue of Liberty with the World Trade Center twin towers, the Empire State Building, and the city in the background was just unbelievable.

Then someone very quietly started singing, "God bless America..." and by the fourth word everyone on deck had joined in. Luckily for all the macho guys it was very dark outside. I don't think there was a dry eye on deck.

That was a memory that would never have happened if it had not been for Ralph and Betty's love and patience in dealing with us while we were struggling with our doubts and fears.

I also realized that the Statue is not a memorial to the weak and timid souls that had been too afraid of the unknown to leave their homes for a new life in a new land. It is not a memorial to the fearful and spineless who had tried to negotiate with the British over taxes. It is not a tribute to the critics who never accomplish anything themselves, but make a life's work out of criticizing the people who are making things happen. It is not a memorial to the gutless wonders that take advantage of everything that this wonderful country has to offer, and then go on television or march in the streets in protest every time the heroic soldiers of this country go into battle to keep this country free, or to help other countries gain their freedom.

That Statue is a tribute to the strong, valiant, courageous, men and women who had the courage to stand up for what they believed in and who were willing to fight to the death for what is good and right, so that millions of people coming after them could have a better life.

It is a shame and a disgrace that the very people who were given that freedom have now turned against the principles they stood for, and that the very things that they fought and died for are not even being taught in our public school system any more. After the country was founded, the weak-minded socialists started coming over and infiltrating the country. The socialistic minded have taken over the school system and have been teaching the children and grandchildren of valiant men and women that war is bad, and that we should never fight against anything or anybody, that we should just embrace every religion, every belief, and every person who wants to come to our country. Even if the purpose in their coming to our country is to destroy our nation and our way of life. I think that it is time for our elected officials to stand up for the Constitution of the United States of America and stop letting the entire country be jerked around by idiotic special interest groups promoting their warped beliefs that are in direct opposition to everything the founding fathers stood for. If a politician won't make a stand for America, let's vote him out of office and replace him with someone with backbone. If we don't make a stand soon, the Constitution will be replaced, the Bill of Rights will be done away with, and the Statue of Liberty will be torn down by the new Dictators who are daily trying to take over our country.

Sorry, those last few paragraphs got off into my personal opinions. But I noticed that as I grew mentally and emotionally and got more of my financial needs taken care of, I found myself caring about things that I had never really thought much about before. I think that we all tend to just go along with the crowd and with what we have been taught until someone comes along and points out the end result of our current thinking and actions. Once it is pointed out to us, we realize that we really don't necessarily agree with the crowd, or with the mass media slant on things, we had just never sat down and thought it through. I think it is time to sit down and think about things before it is too late.

If people start protesting our system because they want to live in a socialist or communist country we should give them two options: Keep quiet, or let them renounce their American citizenship and move to a socialist country where things are already being done the way they are trying to get them done here. But we should not let them take away all of the freedom that valiant men and women have given their lives for.

Playing golf at Poipu Bay, Kauai

Tim & Anna at the Honolulu Hard Rock Cafe

FIFTEEN

Throughout our relationship there were many different teaching methods that Ralph used to change my thinking and to educate me as a business owner. Sometimes he would recommend that I read a specific book and the next time we met we would discuss the concepts in the book and how we could apply them to our lives. He said that all of the wisdom of the ages had been written down somewhere, and our assignment, if we wanted to be wiser, smarter, more successful, etc. was to find the books that held true wisdom, then read, study, and discuss them until we could comprehend and apply that wisdom to our lives.

While we were in Hawaii we had lunch at the Hard Rock Café in Honolulu. They had the car that Elvis had used in the movie 'Blue Hawaii' hanging from the ceiling. I'd never been to a Hard Rock Café before so I found it very interesting. The atmosphere was relaxed, as just about everything in Hawaii is, but the food was excellent.

In our conversation, I questioned the value of paying a certain amount of money for a particular book. The price seemed to be extremely high for one book. His response was, "You're not paying that amount of money for a bunch of white pages with printing on them, bound together in what we call a book. You're paying that ridiculously low amount of money in exchange for about twenty years worth of research by this author on this particular subject. He went and interviewed hundreds of leaders from different fields and then distilled all that information down into the basic fundamental knowledge on the subject. That's what you are paying for. Even if you wanted to, you probably couldn't get in touch with, and go to personally interview even one of those individuals for less money than the price of the book."

I had to agree. "If you look at it that way the book is probably worth a lot more than it is selling for."

He went on, "If you bought it in a used bookstore for a dollar and took it home and never read it, or never applied it to your life, then it wasn't worth it. You wasted a dollar. On the other hand, if you not only read it, but you apply these principals to your life, it will change the results you get, which will dramatically increase your income, and the book will be worth hundreds or thousands of times what you paid for it. A book just stores data or information. To make the information valuable, you have to put it into a brain that can reason. The determining factor in the value of a book is the person who reads it. A book has very little inherent value."

That was a college word I must have missed. "Inherent value, what does that mean?"

"Literally, a book is just a bunch of papers bound together. There are not a lot of things it could be used for. You could use the paper to help start a fire, but that wouldn't justify the price of most books. You could use a book to prop up a projector or you could use it as a doorstop, but you could also use a brick just as effectively for a lot less money. Since there are not a lot of uses for a book outside of reading it, we say that it doesn't have inherent value. Gold, on the other hand has great inherent value because there are literally thousands of practical uses for it. In many applications gold is the absolute best metal that could be used, because of its inherent qualities. So, even outside of its use in coins or jewelry, it still has great value. So we say that it has inherent value. If I were ever going to become a collector, for profit, I would choose to collect things that had inherent value. I would choose gold or silver over baseball cards for example, because of the inherent value of the metal, outside of its value as a collectible item. If you take out the value to a collector, or just the pride of ownership, the only inherent value I can think of for baseball cards would be to clip them onto a kids bicycle wheels to keep them entertained for a while. I'm not putting down people who collect baseball cards, or art, or anything else, because they obviously don't do it for the inherent value. And that's not why I buy books. I buy them because they can change the way I think, they can change my life for the better if I let them."

After we had that conversation, I never looked at books the same way again.

He later told me that whenever you meet someone that is unusually successful in any field, ask him what books he has read. He said that ideas have consequences. So when we see someone with results that are outstanding we should try to find out where the ideas came from that created those results.

Another of Ralph's teaching techniques was to suggest a subject or an idea for me to research on my own and then we would get together to discuss what I had learned from my own research and investigation. I never knew if it was a subject that he threw out at random, or if it was something that he thought I needed to work on. Either way, I learned to take a topic or a comment and learn everything I could about it. I also found out that after I had shared with him what I had learned, that he was going to ask me how I could apply that knowledge to my life, or how does that concept affect my life. So I started figuring the answer out before we met again.

On one occasion he was about to leave town for Europe for several weeks and he said, "I heard a guy named Jim Rohn make a statement one time. I want you to write it down and think about it while I'm gone, and when I return you can tell me what you've learned, or what conclusions you've come to about this statement. Here's the statement. Every human being must suffer either the pain of discipline or the pain of regret. Discipline weighs ounces, regret weighs tons."

For the next few weeks I thought about that as I was going about my daily routine and jotted down some notes. When we got back together and had a moment alone, he said, "Every human being must suffer either the pain of discipline or the pain of regret, what do you think about that?"

(AUTHORS NOTE: I included this chapter to illustrate one of Ralph's teaching techniques, but the opinions expressed from this point on are my own opinions based on my personal observations.)

"Well, first of all, you could probably write a book about the implications and conclusions that could be drawn from that statement. The first thing that came to my mind was the fact that this statement verified what my co-workers used to say when I worked construction. Their attitude toward life was summed up in the phrase, 'Life is a pain, and then you die.' They used a different word than pain, but that's close enough. Of course, since I've been involved in this business, I've come to realize that life is not so much about what happens to you, but how you respond to things that happen to you. I've also learned that we each have a lot more control over what happens to us based on the decisions we make and the actions we take, than most people want to admit."

Ralph said, "That's true. All men are self-made to a certain extent, but only the successful want to take the credit for where they are in life. So what have you learned besides the fact that in life there will be pain?"

"I've figured out that the concept of discipline or regret affects every area of your life, from simple day-to-day things, to major accomplishments or failures. Physically, either you discipline yourself to shower and shave, or you begin to stink and look scraggly and offend everyone around you. You discipline yourself to brush and care for your teeth, or you'll regret it when they rot and fall out. At home you either discipline yourself to take the garbage out regularly, or regret not doing it after it has stunk up the whole house."

"You discipline yourself in changing the oil and doing maintenance on your vehicle, or you regret it when it breaks down and cost you a lot of money to fix. In school, you must discipline yourself to study, or regret it when you fail a class or a grade and have to watch all your friends move on while you become the laughing stock of the younger class. You discipline yourself to drive the speed limit, or regret it when they write you a ticket or take away your license to drive."

As I paused to get my breath, he nodded and said, "Go on."

I said, "You discipline yourself to eat healthy or regret it when your body becomes diseased and weak. You discipline yourself to eat moderately, or you regret it when you become obese, with all the problems that being fat would entail. You discipline yourself to wash your clothes regularly, or regret it when you're in a hurry to get to an important event and have nothing clean to wear. Discipline yourself to get to your job on time and discipline yourself to do what is necessary to accomplish the job, or regret it when you lose your job, your income, and possibly your furniture, your car, and your house."

He was still nodding so I kept going. "With the family, you have to discipline yourself to love and care for the family and develop the relationships, or you regret it when you're spouse leaves you for someone who they believe will love and care for them, or the kids leave home and never want to see you again. Or they start hanging out with the wrong crowd who gives them the attention they crave, and they get involved in drugs or alcohol or worse. Spiritually you discipline yourself now or you'll regret it for a long, long time. You either study the Bible until you understand that there is a God, there is right and there is wrong, and you have to stand up for what is right, or you regret it when your country falls from within like so many others throughout history, into socialism or communism. Then you have a dictator holding a gun to your head and telling you what you can and can't do, what you can say and can't say, totally controlling your life. The concept of discipline or regret applies to individuals, businesses, churches, states, countries, and any group or organization. I read a quote by a guy named Thomas Huxley who said, *'The most valuable result of all education is to make you do the thing you have to do, when it ought to be done, whether you like it or not. It is the first lesson that ought to be learned, and however early a mans training begins, it is probably the last lesson that he learns thoroughly.'* I've also figured out that socialists, communists, and people who believe in false gods are living all over the world, including throughout the United States. Some of them have even managed to get themselves into positions of power and authority in our country. I've learned that they are always actively promoting their evil beliefs and way of life, and if good people don't stand up and make their voice heard, then evil will triumph by default. Not because they are right, or because they are in the majority, but just because the people who believe in the True God, who believe in Capitalism and Free Enterprise, refuse to vote or take an active part in electing good people to run our country."

Ralph could see that I was about to get worked up about politics so he said, "What other areas does this concept apply to?"

"Well, if you are in business for yourself, you must discipline yourself to do everything that needs to be done, or you'll regret it when your business fails. The concept applies extremely well to raising children. All you have to do is to get around people with kids and it becomes very obvious. If the parent doesn't establish rules for the children to follow, the kids very quickly learn that they can do anything they want because there are no rules. If they tell the kids there are rules, but they refuse to enforce them, or refuse to discipline the children, then you get the same result; children that are wild and unruly and have no respect for authority. If children aren't taught to respect the authority of the parents by the time they are six years old, then the cold, cruel world will have to discipline them later. They won't listen to, obey, or respect the authority of teachers in school. They have always gotten what they wanted by yelling, screaming, crying, or throwing a temper tantrum, so they expect to get their way by doing that in school."

"If they manage to get through school because our system has become so politically correct that they will pass children without them learning much of anything, then they will always have trouble keeping a job because the boss will be telling them what to do, how to do it, who to do it with whether they like it or not, and since they have never had to submit to any type of authority to get by, they won't submit to a boss either. So they will have a hard time earning a living. I read where adults have been caught shoplifting, and when asked why they did it, they responded that they wanted the item and couldn't afford it, so they just took it. The guilty party couldn't even understand why the business owner and the police were making such a fuss over it. They've taken what they wanted all their life and there have never been any consequences. Their parents let it go, the schools let it go, the church let it go, so what's the big deal? So people grow up without any discipline and then they get out into the real world and they will get into trouble with the law. They react like they always have by yelling and screaming and showing disrespect for authority, and end up going to jail. Or worse, they act that way with someone just like them, and end up getting killed by that person who wants to get their way and will stop at nothing to get it."

"My conclusion is that if parents do not love their kids enough to discipline them and teach them to respect authority, the vast majority of those children will end up in jail or dead. I think the biggest challenge is because parents don't understand discipline and punishment. Discipline is instructing and teaching a child what he needs to know to be able to have a more successful and rewarding life. Punishment is showing a child that there are consequences to violating the rules or the laws, and giving them a taste of what life will be like if they don't learn discipline. Discipline is done out of love, with restraint. Unfortunately punishment is often done out of anger, and the child doesn't get the correct message. The discipline of a child may be hard, but the regret of not doing it is much worse. If the parents don't discipline the children, the world will discipline them, and the worlds discipline is much more serious, sometimes fatal. If children never learn the lesson of discipline or regret, their entire life will be one painful experience after another. They can't get their way like they did growing up, so they end up losing job after job, getting divorced, turning to alcohol or drugs to try to escape their problems, and its primarily because their parents didn't teach them that you can't always have exactly what you want. Other people have to be taken into consideration, laws of society have to be adhered to, and people in positions of authority should be treated with respect whether you like them personally or not. I realize of course that once people reach the age of accountability they can choose to change and act differently, but still, the parents should be responsible for teaching their children to respect authority and that violating rules will have consequences."

"As I have looked around, I don't see people raising their kids the way I was raised. We were taught that mom and dad were the center of the family and the kids were next in the line of priorities. We didn't have any problem with that once we understood the ground rules. We were each given chores to do and if we didn't work, we didn't eat. So we learned early that there is no free lunch. If you want something, you have to work for it. The first time that each of us kids tried throwing a temper tantrum, because we'd seen our friends get their way by doing that, we got a whipping that we never did forget. I don't know about the others, but I decided that I would not do that again because I definitely did not like the result. That decision has probably kept me out of jail on numerous occasions when I felt like blasting someone, and didn't, because I knew that the end result, or the regret would be much worse. I guess that I was lucky because my parents believed what the Bible says about 'spare the rod and spoil the child'. So, I think that if people raise their kids according to Doctor Crock or some other self-proclaimed expert instead of the Holy Scriptures, their children are in for a rough time."

"Most people today seem to make the kids the center of the universe and let the children think that everything revolves around what the children want to do. Mom and dad will change or adjust their schedules to suit the children. The kids decide where, when, or if the family goes out to eat. The kid's preferences come before the parents on entertainment, and vacations. Those kids are in for a rude awakening when they get out into the real world and have to adapt quickly or else suffer the consequences. I've heard a lot of moms say that they feel like they have given up even having a life, and have been relegated to the job of taxi driver, cook, and maid for the children, and they don't understand how it got that way. I don't think that it is wrong for a mom or dad to do all that because that's what they want to do, but I have heard a lot of people who are living that way, say they do it because that is the way everyone around them is living, and they have essentially become unwilling slaves to their children's desires."

"For example, a few years ago we had a couple in business with us who brought their teenagers to a business convention. After the meeting all the business partners needed to meet to discuss future plans, so we decided where we would go to eat and talk. This couple said that they could not go with us because their kids wanted to go to their favorite restaurant, and they even asked if we could all change our plans and go with them! I wondered to myself, who's wearing the pants in this family? Their financial future is on the line and they are letting their children's eating preferences determine their success or failure!"

I looked back at Ralph and stopped. "I'm sorry, I didn't mean to get up on a soapbox. My conclusion is that as an adult, discipline is something you have to do to yourself, or else you will regret it when the world disciplines you, and the worlds discipline is always much worse. Discipline weighs ounces; regret weighs tons. Each of us *CAN* choose to suffer the pain of discipline, or else we *WILL* suffer the pain of regret."

"And before you ask how this could affect my life, I can tell you that it already has. I find myself doing things immediately that I use to put off until later. I've also noticed that my life is beginning to be less of a pain because there is getting to be less and less regret."

Ralph just looked me in the eye and said, "Very good."

As he walked away I thought, 'That is incredible. He says two words and I feel better about myself than I have felt in years.' I guess that is the power of a true mentor. They can do things for you that no one, or nothing else, can do.

SIXTEEN

We were at a major convention in a coliseum filled with thousands of people. The house lights were out. The spotlights were focused on center stage where Ralph and Betty Autry had just been introduced to a thunderous standing ovation. I had been with them backstage until they were introduced and now I was standing behind the curtain in the dark where I could see them and listen to them. They always seemed to be able to say things that would help everyone in the audience. As they spoke, the audience was so quiet that you could have heard a pin drop.

RALPH SPEAKING:

We're going to be talking about teamwork together as a husband and wife. Facing the triumphs and more importantly I suppose, facing the challenges. I suppose that when we first start thinking of teamwork we think; oh, well, that means becoming the perfect guy, becoming the perfect gal, and living the perfect days, and doing the perfect thing, and things will work out to be a perfect future. But it just doesn't work that way at all. There is no way you can overestimate how good, and how much fun business can be for you when you work as a team. It doesn't mean that every now and then your wife's not going to nag, even though I don't think that's a good idea. It doesn't mean that every now and then your husband's not going to make all the best decisions, even though I think that's a pretty good idea, too. But it does mean that you accentuate each other's strengths, you protect each other's weaknesses, and you use what you've got. You use the cards that have been dealt to you. Do you try to work toward a better hand? Yes! But most important of all, you try to play the one you got to the utmost, and that is enough. I don't know whether I would have made it or not if it hadn't been for the team person I've got in my wife, my lover, and my best friend, Betty.

BETTY SPEAKING:

I feel very lucky to be a woman who is teamed up in life with Ralph, not only building our family, but also building a future, building our careers together. It's true that two heads are better than one, but you know what? Two hearts are better than one. We share our life together. We dream together. We work together. We play together. And I wouldn't take anything for that, and that's what we want for you. We've always built our business together as a team.

RALPH:

There's no such thing, as a couple that cannot become a terrific team. Remember that. There's no such thing, as a couple that cannot become a terrific team. The two of you need to see your dream, your burn, every single day between yourselves, if no one else, but especially yourselves.

I just had to have my freedom. To me, a sailing ship and nice yachts and vessels always represented freedom. We lived in Florida and when times were at their worst, I'd drive up to the marina in a neighboring town, roughly twenty-five to thirty minutes away, sometimes all the way over to the coast, which was a forty-five minute one way trip. But I would do that because those vessels represented freedom to me. It seems like just about every time I did it, it was a slow, cold, drizzly rain. I didn't mind I loved to walk along and to think. Betty learned to understand that. I just had to have my freedom.

When you're talking about problems and challenges, for goodness sakes, don't the two of you dignify them by giving them a personality, nor a home, especially yours.

I would suggest to you as a couple, as a team, that you pick out one song and make it your theme song. We did that. It was a Ronnie Milsap number. It was called, "What a Difference You've Made In My Life." Play it over, and over, and over again. Betty used to play it on the intercom at home while she was taking care of the kids. I'd play it while driving back and forth in the car. We'd play it on the way to meetings. We'd play it on good nights. We'd play it on nights that could have been better; we played it all the time. It should become your theme song.

BETTY:

Ralph says that he can take anything on the outside world as long as he knows that when he comes home and he opens that door and walks in, that I'm on his side, that we're a team, that we can do anything together. I never want to let him down in that area.

I knew that Ralph was out there working hard for Kevin and Susan and for me. We learned to focus on the positive rewards that we knew were going to come and never, ever focus on the temporary challenges that would come our way.

We always gave God thanks, cause everything good comes from Him, and to Him only we give all the glory and all the honor.

RALPH:

You don't have the slightest idea how strong you personally can become. The only thing we know with absolute certainty is that God is bringing us through. He is in control.

You've seen the image of Superman with an S on his chest. Superman is a concept, but it's not real. Take a long hard look at yourself. You are real. The champion within you that can be developed is real. You have within you the seeds of greatness. But you have to be the one to nurture that seed, to develop it, and help it to grow. Reality is what you say it is.

Look at freedom. You're either free or you're not. You've got to have financial freedom before you can have freedom of the heart, freedom of the spirit. You can't mention the word freedom, men, without hearing in the background, coming over the horizon, the thundering hooves of responsibility. Responsibility is what gives birth to freedom, gives it life, sustains, it, and guarantees it for others.

BETTY:

Adversity and challenges are a part of life. The winds of adversity blow in every direction and sooner or later they hit all of our lives. Do not fear the winds of adversity; remember that a kite rises against the wind, rather than with it.

Adversity includes all the difficulties that we go through; all the trials and struggles, heartaches and pain. It comes in all shapes and forms and intensities. It can be the greatest motivation for our growth, if we choose for it to be; or it can be the deadliest form of discouragement if we allow it to be. It all depends on how we respond. Adversity is inevitable; misery is optional. You choose how you will react, or respond to adversity.

It is during the times of your greatest adversity that you learn more about yourself than any other time, and you find out how much courage you really have, and you find out that you are much stronger than you thought you were.

RALPH:

Leaders look at what they are going to; not what they are going through. Average people never accomplish much in life because they focus on what they are going through; their circumstances, situations, challenges, etc. They get all bogged down with where they are. If leaders don't like where they are, they focus on where they want to be and start moving in that direction.

People who accomplish great things in life had the same circumstances, situations, and challenges that others had. Winners use these as their motivation to move on. Losers use them as their excuses for not moving on.

Losers say, "I can't because I don't have time."

Winners say, "I don't have enough time in my life to do the things I want, therefore I will accomplish such and such so that I will have time." Winners realize that we all make time to do the things that we really want to do.

The person who doesn't have time to help coach a little league team is the same person who will spend three to four hours a day watching television.

Losers say, "I can't accomplish anything because I don't have any money."

Winners say, "I don't have any money, therefore I will get out and accomplish something so that I will have the money I need."

Losers say, "I can't build a business in addition to working my job because I have kids that I want to spend time with."

Winners say, "I have kids that I want to spend time with, so my children will be my motivation for building a business in addition to my job, so that one day I can quit working a job and have forty to sixty hours a week to spend with my family."

Losers say, "I can't build a business on the side because when I get home from work I'm tired."

Winners say, "When I get home from work I'm tired, and I don't want to do that for the rest of my life, so I'm going to build a business to the point that I can quit my job."

Winners and losers all have the same amount of time, they all have financial challenges, family situations, problems, career challenges, etc. The difference in those who get where they want to go on the road of life and those who get run over by life is simply a matter of attitude.

Winners say, "I'm going to make something happen."

Losers say, "I'm going to wait and see what happens." Even if you are on the right road, if you just stand there, you are going to get run over. Ultimately we are each responsible for where we are in life, because we are where we are based on decisions that we have made and actions that we have taken, or failed to take.

Betty and I decided early in our marriage that as a team, we wanted to make a difference in other peoples lives...

And then Ralph was telling the story of the old man walking down the beach and putting starfish back in the water. I remembered him telling me the story on the beach in San Destin about ten years before, and I remembered relating to the young boy playing happily on the beach who had asked the old man what difference it would make, because I hadn't seen much sense in it either.

And then as my eyes got moist and teary it suddenly dawned on me; I wasn't the young boy playing happily on the beach, content with life when Ralph had come along. I was a starfish. I was lost and alone with no hope of a better life ahead. I was very quickly drying up in my spirit and the joy of life was draining away. Like thousands or perhaps millions of others who had been washed up on the shore by the storms of life, only to see their hopes and dreams whither and die. But unlike others, who seem to be content to accept defeat and to live out their lives of quiet desperation, I had gone searching for help.

Then Ralph had taken me very gently from the helpless, self-centered creature that I was, and had shown me how to not only survive, but to prosper, by being of service to other people.

Perhaps Ralph was not as well known to the general public as

Mother Teresa, or Mahatma Gandhi, or some others, and he may not have made as much of a difference in the world as a whole, as some others have made, but he made a difference to this one. He changed my life forever, and I will be eternally grateful.

One of my goals for the future is to have as much of an impact on at least a few other peoples lives as he had on mine.

Of course, if we were literally dealing with starfish, then I could help them whether they wanted me to help them or not. But in dealing with human beings, I have found that one of the greatest frustrations of life comes when you find someone who needs help and you know that you can help them, so you offer to help, and you get rejected. They won't help themselves, and they won't let anyone else help them. They have decided that misery will be their lot in life, and no one is going to change that. It is very difficult for me to sit by and watch peoples lives slowly deteriorate and fall apart when I know that the answers they need are available. But when they won't accept help when it is offered, much less ask for it, then there doesn't seem to be much that we can do. So the people I help will be the few who are willing to come and ask for help. The ones who are willing to listen, learn, change, grow, and get out of their comfort zone; just as I had to do.

Our world is in serious need of more people who will serve as mentors. Yes, it is frustrating at times, but the few lives that you touch and change forever will make it worth all the time and effort. I encourage you first of all, if you are not where you want to be in life, to start searching for a mentor yourself. The answers to virtually all of this life's problems can be found in books, and the answer to most all of life's problems can be found in the Bible. Whether you consider yourself to be religious or not, I recommend reading it to see how you can have a better life.

Then I would encourage you to become a mentor to others. Be willing to share whatever knowledge you have that will help others to have a happier, more satisfying and productive life.

Ralph Autry on stage with a crowd of 30,000

⟳ · CHAPTER · ⟲

SEVENTEEN

I was headed home from Huntsville, Alabama where I had been taking care of some business. It was about a two-hour drive and it was now close to midnight. That's when the phone call came. It hit me like an unexpected punch in the gut that shocks you and takes your breath away. Ralph Autry had a malignant tumor in his upper chest the size of a grapefruit that was inside and outside his lungs and wrapped around his aorta. It was inoperable.

Suddenly everything that was going on in my life became irrelevant. Everything that was normally on my mind just seemed to fade away. I don't remember anything about the drive home but somehow I made it back. I don't think I accomplished much of anything for a while because nothing seemed to matter. I was just kind of going through the motions of life in a daze.

The next time I saw Ralph he greeted me with a big smile and a firm handshake like nothing was different, "Hey man, how ya' doin?"

He was in a better mood than I was. "I'm okay, tell me about this tumor." In the years that I had known Ralph through all kinds of challenges and obstacles, I had never heard him admit to having a problem. I'd heard him say many times, to many people, "If its not cancer, its not a problem."

He said, "The doc says I have a problem, so they're going to do a bunch of tests and figure out how to attack it."

Typical Ralph; gather intelligence, get the relevant facts, then attack. He made me promise that I would not let his problem slow me down in the pursuit of my life's dreams, or in building my business.

The tumor was malignant and very aggressive, and already at an advanced stage when they found it. The doctors put his body through every form of chemical torture known to man, and then tried some experimental stuff. He never complained. He never expressed anger at the unfairness of it all. He continued to live his life according to his beliefs, as he always had. He proved to the world that he was, in fact, the man that we all thought that he was. He went through the fire and was proven to be good and pure.

I won't try to describe the pain and suffering of the family or the many lives that he had touched. He fought the cancer for eighteen months before the disease took him away. It never beat him. It just took him into the next realm. You cannot beat someone who refuses to ever give up, who will never surrender, who has the heart and soul of a conqueror.

Ralph was not afraid to die. In fact, he was looking forward to meeting his creator and his savior. He said that he had a list of questions that he wanted to ask of his heroes in the Bible. He held on to life because he loved life and he loved his family, and didn't want to see them hurt. But in the end, he just figured that the good Lord needed him somewhere else more than he needed him here.

So Ralph is physically gone from our presence, but his spirit lives on in the hearts and minds of the many people with whom he made a difference.

~ ᴄ ʜ ᴀ ᴘ ᴛ ᴇ ʀ ~

EIGHTEEN

Transcript of Ralph Autry's Funeral Service

Eulogy By Steve Peden:

We're gathered here together in the stillness of the late summer afternoon to remember and to celebrate the life of Ralph Autry. I've known Ralph a long time and when I read through this obituary, it's the first time I've noticed his middle name. Ralph Perrington Autry, Junior was born December 31, 1938 and died September 12, 1998. He leaves in his immediate family, his wife, his son, his daughter, his mother, a sister, one niece, and two nephews. We've come here this afternoon to mourn his passing from our company, to comfort his wife and children and the rest of his family as best we can, as best we know how, and to rejoice. To rejoice in the fact that Ralph has begun a new existence in a far better place than our finite minds can conceive. I know for a fact that Ralph believed that this world is just a shadow of things to come. I can say unequivocally, I can say that I believe that Ralph's faith is now sight.

Words are never sufficient to assuage the sense of loss and words are never really adequate to denote the worth of a good man's life. I want to say to Betty and Kevin and Susan that you have honored me by asking me to speak this day. And I wish that I had the words that could take away all of it, but then that's not the way things are. I feel, very keenly, an inadequacy to stand here and to say exactly what this man has meant to me. And I couldn't possibly say what he's meant to each of you. Words won't allow us to do that.

But Betty and Susan and Kevin, I want you to know, and I know that you know, that all the words that have been said to you in these past two days, that have been said today, that will be said in the coming weeks, behind all of these words are concern; and hearts, grieving hearts, concerned for you, hearts that are grieving with you and for you. And these people who have said these things love you and they want you to know that, and they'll be there if you need them.

In time a monument will be erected over Ralph's grave. It will give his name. It will give the date of his birth and it will give the date of his death. And this monument made of stone will give few, if any other details about this man's life. And if time continues, years from now people are going to pass that grave and see this monument, see the name and see the dates. And these folks are not going to have any inkling, not one inkling about the greatness and goodness of this man. Ultimately though, time and the elements will efface that stone. The name will become fainter and the date will become fainter. But a larger and a more enduring monument than that stone monument has already been erected. It's already been built and it is composed of the influence and the memory of Ralph Autry. The influence that this good man has had in so many lives will continue to be shared and felt in so many other lives for so many years to come that we can't tell where that influence stops. Ralph was a teacher. He just never bothered to get into a school. But I've seen him teach and I've seen him work with people. It is said that a teachers' influence doesn't stop, that it goes on for eternity, and so it is, I think, with him. All of the occasions that he spent helping others, of sharing the faith that he had in God, of encouraging others, whether it be in their religious life or their business life, of just doing things for others, all of those things, over all of these years, Ralph was building his own monument. He built that monument patiently and he built it steadily over the years, in his family life, in his business life, and I think in that pervasive Christ like example that he demonstrated to all men. He has erected a monument of influence and memories. Each of you, over the coming months and days and years, will have occasion to remember the specifics of the influence that he had in your life. If you're here today you can't pass beyond that. He has had an influence on you. John Dunn, the English poet, said "Any mans death demises me, for I am involved in mankind." And he meant by that that all of us are a part of each other. I believe that also. When we remember his work ethic, when we remember his unflagging optimism, when we remember his kindness in word and deed, all of these are a part of the monument Ralph has already built, and has left for us. Ralph's legacy will pass on through his children, and to their children, to succeeding generations. His friends and his business associates will remember his life and they'll pass along the blessing that they found in him and that aspect of his life also. His Christian brothers and sisters will remember the dedication and the faith that he carried right to the last breath of his life. He has influenced the eternities of so many of us by his teaching and by his works and by his example that we can't help but see that monument that he's built. People all over the world, literally all over the world, are better for having known him. So then Ralph's most enduring monument will be that memory in the hearts and in the minds of those that loved him and knew him. And all of us again will pause at some time or another to reflect on his life, some little thing about his life. What the poet Woodsworth said was, "The best portion of a good man's life; his little, nameless, unremembered acts of kindness and love." No doubt, many of us will remember Ralph as, or in the words of the poet Whitman, (Whitman eulogized Lincoln, but I think it applies here,) when we call Ralph the "kindest, wisest soul of all my days and years."

But when I think of the life of Ralph Autry, I think of the more concise and I think the most touching epitaph that anyone ever shared, anyone ever had. It's not printed on a cemetery. It's printed in the book of Genesis. The writer of Genesis said of the man Enoch, that "Enoch walked with God, and Enoch was not for God took him." That's about all that was said about Enoch in this passage. "Enoch walked with God, and Enoch was not for God took him." The details of Enoch's life are not given. What he did from day to day, his family life, his work life, what he enjoyed, the type of parent he was, the type of husband he was, all those things are omitted. And yet the writer sums it up by saying, "Enoch walked with God." Most of us know what Ralph did from day to day. We know his family life. We know what he did for his work life. We know the things he enjoyed, the type of parent and husband he was, and yet I think his life could be summed up the same way Enoch's was. I think Ralph walked with God. I think he was God's man in everything he said and did. I think Ralph walked with God with constancy and a dedication, and a perseverance that frankly puts me to shame. His manner of life, his work ethic, and his faith were so intertwined that the man was a most amazing whole person. Everything, I think, in his life sprang from the fact that he was God's man first. Ralph walked with God. And when this disease struck him, he was still God's man. He was strong and he was courageous in the face of all the pain he had to endure. He was prayerful and he was faithful in adversity.

Truly his life has been a blessing. And even his passing has been a benediction. Betty shared with me, a little while ago, the type of person you know Ralph to be. Ralph left a lot of paperwork for Betty. He even marked the things that were important. And stuck to the table under all the paperwork was a little post-it sticker with a note to Betty. And it said, "It is well with my soul."

So now he is past from our midst. He is not in our presence anymore and what we have left are the memories, and the remembering has begun. His passing leaves us with conflicting emotions; with sadness and with grief for his absence, with thankfulness for the exemplary life that he lived, and most of all with joy, with joy for the reward that he has. The family's grief is that a husband and a father is gone. And our world is a lesser place for his absence and a richer place for having known him.

EULOGY BY DON BASSETT *

I'd like to draw your attention to the 15th Psalm and ask you to reflect with me for a moment on whether or not such a psalm as this does not describe the character of a man like Ralph Autry. "Lord, who shall abide in thy tabernacle? Who shall dwell safely in thy holy hill? He that walketh uprightly and worketh righteousness and speaketh the truth in his heart. He that backbiteth not with his tongue, nor doeth evil to his neighbor, nor taketh up a reproach against his neighbor in whose eyes evil practices are condemned. But he honoreth them that fear the Lord. He sweareth to his own hurt and changeth not. He putteth not out his money for usury nor taketh reward against the innocent. He that doeth these things shall never me moved."

In Psalms 112 , the psalmist says, "Praise ye the Lord. Blessed is the man that feareth the Lord, that delighteth greatly in his commandments, his seed shall be mighty upon earth. The generation of the upright shall be blessed. Wealth and riches shall be in his house and his righteousness endureth forever. Unto the upright there ariseth light in the darkness. He is gracious and full of compassion and righteousness. A good man sheweth favor and lendeth; he will guide his affairs with discretion. Surely he shall not be moved forever. The righteous shall be an everlasting remembrance."

Those psalms are written about people of great character. Ralph was a man suited for greatness. And he met the requirements the word of God stipulates and sets forth for the achievement of greatness. In some respects he achieved that greatness in terms that the world in general would describe as greatness. Steve has made known, has reminded us that there are people all over the world today who have cause to be grateful they have known Ralph and Betty Autry, have benefited greatly from their efforts, and their outlook in many different ways. It has been approximately three years ago that my wife, Nancy, and I were riding in a taxicab in the city of Amsterdam. The taxicab driver was an interesting fellow. He wanted to talk quite a bit. He was from Italy, and I asked him, "How is it that you are a taxicab driver in Amsterdam here in the Netherlands, and you are an Italian National?" He said, "Well, I'm here, of course, on a work permit." And I said, "Oh, you've come up here to drive a taxi." He said, Well, actually there's another business that I'm much more interested in." He began telling me some things describing his business and I said, "You're an Independent Business Owner, aren't you?" He said, "Yes." And I said, "Do you know Ralph and Betty Autry?" He turned around and looked at me and almost ran off the road! He said, "Yes! Do you know Ralph and Betty Autry? They're famous all over Europe!"

Well, I knew Ralph and Betty were well known, highly respected and loved in their business in this country. And for other reasons and as a consequence of their association with many other people on many other basis; church, family and many things that Steve has already brought to our attention. I didn't know they were famous in Europe, but they were. That man had met Ralph and Betty Autry and it changed his life! How many people are there all over the world today who could listen to one of us read Psalm 15 or Psalm 112 and say, "Do you know Ralph Autry? Why that's a description of that man."

Ralph had the seeds of greatness in him and, of course, achieved greatness in business, but also achieved greatness as a father to his children, as a husband to his Betty. And to those of us who knew him in connection with our weekly worship at church, great in good cheer, great in godliness, perhaps greatest of all in prayer. Those of us who have prayed along with him will never forget how we felt when Ralph stepped to the podium to lead us in prayer. It was an unusual experience. It was a God-directed experience. But it was also a very refreshing one for all of us who were there and heard the words he uttered on our behalf before the throne of God. He achieved greatness by the world's standards, immense success. I have thought also about other avenues through which, I believe in due time, he would have extended the use of his talents; already did in many respects.

He was a director of a small organization, which I am a part, called the Biblical Resource Center and Museum. What sort of energies he would have poured into that organization, how much he would have achieved through it along with Betty's help, I do not know. I know only that those of us who are a part of that particular program today are experiencing a sense of irreparable loss. I have often wondered if Ralph would not ultimately have gone into full time evangelistic work. There are those of you who are here this morning, who have known him in a business capacity who might be willing to say, "He already was in full time evangelistic work." And that's so. Steve has said that he was God's man first. And that's right. That always came first in absolutely every aspect of his dealings, with his family, his fellow man, his fellow Christians, his business associates, and consequently, his life constituted an on-going evangelistic effort. Of him, it may be said, as the Lord requested his disciples, that he let his light so shine, that men seeing his good works glorified not him, but his Father who is in Heaven. And for that, we may all be grateful today. And many of us to an extent that would lead us to say, "I owe him my soul."

That raises a question in which I have been wrestling for months now, and I know many of you have too. And that is, "Why?" Why in the very summer of his years, at the point of maximum influence, at the point of maximum yield in terms of investment, of all of that effort of goodness, kindness, steadfast patience, encouragement, proclamation of the word of God, humble and meaningful prayer, should he be taken from among us? It will not do for us to pretend specifically that we may say that we have the answer and that none other may be suggested.

There are things that are kept within the immutable and inscrutable council of God that we do not understand now and may or may not be fully explained to us later on. And the things that belong to God we must leave to God.

But I would like to suggest something to you that has been of some comfort to me over the last several months, as I tried to come to grips with what seems to me something that should not have happened. In James the fifth chapter and verse 10, James, the Lord's brother, I think, wrote, "Take, my brethren, the prophets who have spoken in the name of the Lord for an example of suffering and affliction and of patience." The prophet Jeremiah ministered for forty years and he was called 'the weeping prophet' because there was not much for him to do but preach and weep. His life was one of hardship and affliction and there was scarce little to rejoice about in all of his career. James says to take him as an example of suffering and affliction and of patience. Then James says, "Behold we count them happy who endure. You have heard the patience of Job and have seen the end of the Lord, that the Lord is very pitiful and of tender mercy." The book that bears his name tells us that he did not understand, and that he believed that it was unfair, that as he sat in sack-cloth and ashes and scraped the scabs from his boils with potsherds and listened to his friends criticize him and looked heavenward and asked for an answer and was never given it, day after day after day, possibly year after year after year. I do not know why. But I'm suggesting that from generation to generation God takes special people who are particularly talented and influential, great and mighty men and women, concerning whom, we would say, "They have been selected of God to rise to the heights. Before they leave this earth, they will be presidents. Before they leave this earth, they will preach to millions. Before they leave this earth, they will govern the countries of this world." And then when we think it least appropriate they are stricken with incurable suffering and linger over long months and years and die in their sufferings. They're special people. God has chosen them to the ministry of suffering. God has chosen them to serve as an example of suffering and affliction and of patience, James says. God selected Ralph to step into the ranks of the truly great and practice the ministry of suffering, to leave us an example of suffering and affliction and of patience. In selecting Ralph for that noble number, he selected Ralph to stand in the ranks with his only beloved son.

The apostle Peter wrote, "Hereunto you were called because Christ also suffered for you, leaving you an example that you should follow in his steps. Who did no sin, neither was guile found in his mouth, who when he suffered threatened not, who when he was reviled, reviled not again but committed himself to him that judgeth righteously. Who himself in his own body bear our sins on a tree, that we having died unto sin might live unto righteousness." It is a severe mercy. It is a harsh mercy and it is a severe and demanding, an agonizing honor that God confers upon a few of the truly great, to whom he commits the ministry of suffering. All of us are cut to the heart today that God saw fit to confer that great honor upon Ralph.

But who among us today will not leave here better for that great ministry that he practiced. We needn't weep for him. He may say with the apostle Paul, "The time of my departure is come. I have fought a good fight. I have finished my course. I have kept the faith, and henceforth there is laid up for me a crown of righteousness which the Lord, the righteous judge, shall give me that day and not to me only, but unto all them also that loved his appearing."

Let us walk in the steps of his example and join him someday, where we'll sing forever before the throne of God, the great songs that Ralph loved. Shall we pray.

Almighty God, our Heavenly Father, we offer you our thanks on this day for the wonderful example of this good man, for the unflagging courage that he showed in the face of suffering, for the good cheer that he always exhibited, though in pain, he passed his days. For the increasing love that he showed for thee and for thy Son, and for the saving gospel truth for which the savior died. For the intense love and the loving remembrance that he left to Betty and to Kevin and to Susan and to his mother. For all those wonderful memories that he offered out of his tears, out of his suffering and out of that long period during which he practiced that special ministry given to those few great men, like Jeremiah, and Job and your own beloved Son, Jesus. Please watch over, dear Father, those of us who must remain behind and mourn him. Especially we pray today for Betty and for Kevin and Susan and for Ralph's mother and for the extended family all today who are grief-stricken over what in our estimation is a premature departure from this life. But in your great plan and in your great wisdom, a part of that great scheme of redemption in which we may all rejoice someday at the coming of your Son. We pray that you will watch us all through this day. Help us to do your will. Help us to be of whatever comfort we can to those who are most intensely struck by the sadness of this day. And then watch over us as we leave this place, and help us to accept our lives as a ministry, as an occasion, as an opportunity for service to thee and to others, as Ralph did, is our prayer in the name of the Savior. Amen.

*In addition to being a very close personal friend of Ralph's, Don Bassett is the Chairman and CEO of the Biblical Resource Center & Museum in Memphis, Tennessee. The Center is a non-profit, non-denominational organization that is helping people to discover the world of the Bible by offering:

Exhibits, including Ancient artifacts and replicas
Adult lectures
Archaeological Digs
Mummy Workshops
Bible Story Times
Bible Lab- a self paced study of the Bible
Educational tours for children or adults
A Library- books, CD's, videos, tapes, etc.
A Museum Store- educational material
Tours to ancient Biblical sites, and more.

For more information on the Biblical Resource Center & Museum go to: **www.biblical-museum.org**

Ralph & Betty Autry were Charter Members of the organization and believed that educating people about the Bible, where it came from, and how we got it, would make a difference in peoples lives. They would encourage you to help support this worthy endeavor. If you liked this book, (or even if you didn't) please consider making a donation to this educational organization in honor of Ralph & Betty Autry and let them know you heard about them through this book.

Tim & Anna (far right) next to Ralph & Betty
at the Rainbow Room atop the NBC Tower, New York City

Ralph, Anna and Tim on stage at a regional convention

Mentor

Protegé

· CHAPTER ·

NINETEEN

How To Be A Great Student or Protégé

As I became more aware of the need for people to have a mentor in their lives I began putting together a list of things that I believe will help you to be a better student, or protégé.

(NOTE FROM THE AUTHOR: The word 'protégé' is probably a better word to use than 'student', but I was not familiar with the word protégé until the last few years. Also, protégé seems to insinuate an exclusive relationship between the teacher and student. My relationship with Ralph was not exclusive. I was only one of many people that he taught, so I use the word 'student' because that is how I thought of myself.)

A great student will search until he finds a Mentor who is not only capable, but also *willing* to work with him to bring out the greatness that is hidden inside every one of us. Not all successful people are willing to mentor others. Just because you are successful in finding someone who *could* help you, doesn't guarantee that they will be *willing* to help you. If they absolutely refuse to help you, then find someone else who is not only capable, but also willing.

Mentors come in all shapes, sizes, ages, and from all different races, religions, education levels, and backgrounds. As you search for a mentor, you will not be able to determine whether or not a person will be a good mentor by just looking at those things. A great student will look at the results, accomplishments, or achievements that potential mentors have displayed in their lives and then decide whether or not those results would be worth emulating before considering a person as a mentor.

A great student will find a mentor who can point out the books that will help them the most, thereby saving them years of worthless reading. The greatest wisdom of the ages may be found in books, but finding it amongst the millions and millions of books available could take several lifetimes. It is much easier to find a good mentor who can not only teach you personally, but can also suggest reading selections that will benefit you the most.

To be a great student you will need to understand that you must *pursue* the relationship with the mentor, because you are the one who stands to benefit the most from the relationship. Don't expect for a mentor to act like a supervisor and come looking for you to 'teach you something'. It is up to you to find them and ask questions. Ralph said that if he acted like my boss and just told me what to do, then I would continue to think like an employee. Even if I did the work, my thinking would not change, and he wanted me to learn to think like a business owner.

A great student asks lots of questions and then listens and takes notes. There is no way anyone can remember everything they hear. Studies show that we only retain about ten percent of what we hear for over twenty-four hours. Take notes now, and the power of the truths being taught will become clearer as you grow.

A great student is not ashamed to put himself into a subservient position to the mentor, even if the mentor is younger than the student, or the opposite gender.

A great student will always ask the mentor's advice before making any major decision. This does not mean that you always have to do what the mentor suggests, but you do want to at least get his input on the situation just in case he can see something from his perspective, or from previous experience, that you can't see.

A great student wants to know what the mentor has learned; he doesn't just want what the mentor has. If you just get what he has, you can lose it. If you learn what he has learned, you can get what he has and more.

A great student will invest whatever time and money is necessary to be in the presence of the mentor as much as possible. The easier you make the mentor's life, the more the mentor will be willing to go out of his way to help you. What you receive back will be worth many times more than what you gave. Maybe the mentor can afford to pay for the lunch much easier than you can afford to, but if you can find out in one hour what has taken the mentor many years to learn, it is worth the price of a meal.

A great student will bounce new ideas off the mentor before implementing them into his own life or business. Many times what we think is a brilliant idea has been tried before and failed. Asking first can avoid a lot of wasted time and money.

A great student will always edify and support his mentor in public. If you disagree with them, ask questions in private about why they believe what they believe.

A great student will tell his mentor what he wants from the relationship and what he is willing to do in exchange for it.

A great student will be honest with the mentor. A mentor can only give you good advice if the facts that you give him are accurate. He already knows that you are not perfect; so don't try to act like you don't have any challenges.

A great student will be loyal to his mentor. When others, who are not your mentor, see the respect and admiration your mentor receives from you, they may try to gain some of your respect for themselves, by saying something like, "Let's get together some time. I think I know some things that would be beneficial to you. " Be very careful of people like this. Their motive is not to help you, but to gain recognition for themselves. Personal advice without a close personal relationship can be very dangerous, even if they actually do have good intentions.

A great student realizes that he will become more and more like the people he spends most of his time with, and will therefore strive to spend most of his time with people that he would like to become more like.

A great student will always be listening for the purpose of improving himself. Too many people listen, but hear only what they think would improve their spouse, or someone else. Always be asking yourself, "How does this apply to ME? How can I improve myself?"

A great student will listen and learn with an open mind, and a willingness to change. Too many people listen only to find facts that verify what they already believe, and disregard the rest. Don't let your mind become like concrete, 'all mixed up and permanently set'. What you already believe has gotten you to where you are in life. To move on you may have to gain some new beliefs.

A great student realizes that learning is a lifelong process, and won't let frustration set in when he doesn't see the results he wants immediately.

A great student will learn to focus on what he wants, until he gets it. The story is told of tigers in Africa that pick out one gazelle to focus on, and then they charge, knowing that they can outrun and kill the gazelle in a short chase. If the hunter maintains the 'eye of the tiger' it will catch and kill its prey. The gazelles know this, so as soon as a tiger charges, other gazelles will dart in-between the tiger and his prey to try and distract him. If that one succeeds, another gazelle will run between the tiger and its new prey, distracting the tiger off into a new direction. Before long the tiger has expended its energy and has caught nothing. Don't let life's many distractions come between you and your chosen goal. Focus on one goal until you have achieved it, then decide on the next, and by so doing you will accomplish much more than the people who are always 'busy' but never seem to catch anything. Don't confuse activity with accomplishment.

A great student will be willing to share his newfound knowledge with others who are willing to listen and learn. We learn best what we teach others. Therefore, a great student will soon find himself in the role of a mentor for others.

Son Kevin and Betty with Robert Kiyosaki,
Best Selling Author of the Rich Dad Series of Books

TWENTY

HOW TO BE A GREAT MENTOR

Since I became aware of the need for more mentors in America and the world, I have been doing an in-depth study of mentoring. The following is a list of observations I have made and some of the characteristics that I believe will help you to be a better mentor. They are not in any particular order as far as priority or importance. Some of them may not apply to your particular situation and there could probably be many more characteristics added for different occupations and fields of endeavor. My hope is that you will begin a study of your own to see how you can become a better Mentor as well as a better Protégé.

A great mentor will never give advice to a student until he knows the student very well personally. He will want to know what the student wants to have and what he wants to do with his life. He will want to know his likes and his dislikes, and his attitude toward many different things before he gives any advice. Essentially a great mentor knows that he can't give you good directions until he knows where you are and where you want to go.

A great mentor will never try to force his opinions or beliefs on a student. If asked, he will explain why he believes a certain way, but he will allow the student to decide for himself what he wants to believe. Ralph told a story about the father who told his son to sit down several times and the child defiantly continued standing. Finally the dad went over, put his hands on his son's shoulders and pushed him down into the chair. The son looked up defiantly and said, "I may be sitting down on the outside, but on the inside I'm still standing!" A man convinced against his will is of the same opinion still.

To be a great mentor read continuously in your field of expertise so that you will continue to grow personally, and also so that you will know whether or not any particular book would help your protégés. Recommend the books that will most likely help them change their lives for the better.

Never try to bluff a student. You could end up giving them bad advice. If you don't know something, then admit it, and move on. A great mentor doesn't know everything about everything, he just passes on what knowledge he does have to those who are seriously interested.

The difference in a life of poverty and a life of wealth is knowledge and wisdom. A great mentor can pass on a lifetime of knowledge and wisdom to a good student, and move them from poverty to wealth in a relatively short period of time. Just make sure that you are teaching from knowledge and experience, not guesswork or theory. Teach what you know or have done personally, not what you have read about or heard about.

The closer your relationship is to your student, the more you can teach them. You don't have to spill your guts and tell them all of your flaws, but don't try to hide behind a curtain of perfection. Let them see that you, too, have not only hopes and dreams, but also challenges, and frustrations like everyone else. Hopefully by the time you are in a mentoring position you will have learned how to deal with those things positively and can teach others.

Mentors fall into different categories. You may find yourself in several categories.

Parents: teach children the basics of how to live. How to eat, drink, put on clothes, cleanliness and grooming, how to use a telephone, tie your shoe laces, and thousands of other things that we, as adults, take for granted because we have done them for so long that we have forgotten that someone had to take the time and effort to teach us, otherwise we would not know how to do them today. There are probably hundreds of things that you should thank your parents for. To be a better parent, realize that kids don't come into the world knowing all the things that you now take for granted; it is your responsibility to teach them.

Preachers and Teachers: teach us spiritual values and the basics of education. Not all Pastors, Ministers, or Professors are mentors, but some of them are very good ones. We should all be thankful to teachers and ministers who have helped to educate us. They have tough jobs that usually don't pay very well.

Career: Many people, who have worked their way up a corporate ladder to a successful position, had someone who 'showed them the ropes', of how to fit into the system, and work their way up. School doesn't teach you everything you need to know to get ahead in the real world. The challenge to *being* a good mentor in the corporate world is that you may be training your replacement. The challenge to *finding* a good mentor in the corporate world is that most people higher up the corporate ladder have a fear of training their replacement, and are hesitant to teach people everything they know.

Entrepreneurial: Most successful business owners had a successful business owner as a mentor or guide. Very few schools teach you anything about owning your own business, much less about how to succeed in an entrepreneurial venture. If schools do propose to teach you about business, a professor who has no personal business experience typically teaches the course, and will be teaching theories from a textbook written by a professor, not a business owner. (Go back to the lesson on taking advice from people with 'fruit on the tree'.)

A great mentor will see a students faults and weaknesses long before the student does. He will then try to help the student to avoid the pitfalls that those weaknesses could cause.

A great mentor will be continually stretching a student out of their comfort zone, until they are confident in just about any situation, with any group of people.

A great mentor would rather see someone succeed and not like him, than to have someone like him, and not succeed. He will tell the truth whether the student likes it or not. Friends will sometimes avoid saying things that will hurt your feelings, or cause you to not like them, even if telling you would be in your best interest.

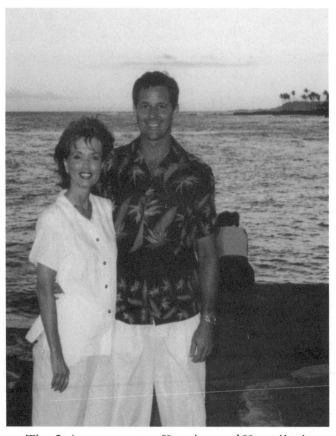

Tim & Anna, sunset on Kauai, second Hawaii trip

Tim & Anna introducing Ralph's mentor,
Jerry before his famous 'Come On' speech

— · CHAPTER · —

TWENTY-ONE

There were many things that Ralph Autry did for me that I didn't realize until years later, looking back. He got me involved in life, in competition, in new adventures, in exploring new places and new activities. He taught me about heroes and how having heroes will make you a better person because you want to become more like them. He taught me that a man needs a battle to fight, he needs a challenge to face, and he needs an enemy to attack. He awakened in me the fierce qualities of a warrior that all men are born with, which get beaten out of most of us while we are still children. Then he helped me to channel that energy into productive activities that would benefit my family and myself. He released me from my cage and let me know that it's okay to come out and do some exciting things. Exciting doesn't have to be dangerous; it just has to be something new, or something outside of your comfort zone. In a civilized society we don't have to take up a sword to fight off invading enemies, but we do have to attack our own fears and overcome our own inhibitions in order to prevail in the business world so that we can provide well for our families.

Ralph believed that the Bible is the inspired word of God, that Jesus was the only true Son of God, that Jesus willingly laid down his life as a sacrifice so that anyone who believed on him and obeyed the conditions that he had set forth as being necessary to receive God's grace could be saved. Ralph had done what he believed the Bible stipulates as being necessary. He had heard the word of God, believed it, repented of his sins, confessed his sins, and had been immersed in baptism in the name of the Father, the Son and the Holy Spirit, just as the Bible clearly teaches. So, according to the scriptures, he had followed the pattern, his sins were washed away, and he continued to live his life according to the Word, therefore he could look forward to an eternal life in Heaven. As he said, "If you know the final score, you don't sweat the ups and downs between the starting point and the final buzzer."

Ralph said that some people would take a single phrase from the Bible and base their whole hope of salvation on that one verse. For example, "If you only believe, you shall be saved." That's like someone discussing the recipe of a cake, and whether or not you need to use eggs in the recipe. So one person says, "If you will only use eggs, you will get a good cake." While they are correct that eggs are necessary, that doesn't mean that eggs are the **only** ingredient necessary. You can do whatever you want with eggs only, but if you don't add any other ingredients, you will never have a cake. The Bible says that even the demons *believe*, and tremble. But the demons aren't saved because there are other conditions necessary besides believing. You can't just pull one verse out of context and ignore the rest of the entire Bible and expect to be pleasing to God. We may not completely understand everything there is to know in the Bible, but we do know that if a person's belief on a subject contradicts other verses in the Bible, then that person's belief is incorrect. You have to accept the entire Word of God to be acceptable.

True belief will cause a person to *obey* the Word, and *do* whatever it says to do, to qualify to receive God's grace and obtain salvation. You cannot earn your salvation, but you do have to obey the Word to put yourself into a position where you can receive God's grace. So Ralph encouraged everyone to study the Bible and to meet all of the terms and conditions that are stipulated, instead of picking and choosing which ones you wanted to comply with, and which ones you wanted to leave out just because another person told you that this one or that one is not necessary, or because you didn't understand the reasoning behind the condition.

I realize that Ralph's political, family, business, and religious beliefs may be different from many of the readers of this book. God made us all free moral agents, which means that you can choose to believe whatever you choose to believe based on whatever criteria you choose. But this book was written about Ralph Autry and some of the things I learned from him. He knew that there had to be an absolute standard of right and wrong, otherwise the entire world would be chaos. If there were no absolute standard, then everyone would be free to murder, rob, rape, lie, cheat, steal, etc. and no one could tell anyone else not to, because one persons opinion is no better than another persons opinion. Ralph believed the Bible to be the standard that humans were to live by, and so he studied it with an open mind and came to his own conclusions based on the scriptures. He knew what he believed and why he believed it and he stood firm in his beliefs. He would encourage you to do the same. Don't leave your eternal destination to chance. Get the facts about the Bible, not opinions, develop strong beliefs, and then live by them.

Ralph was a man of principle and integrity. He lived his life according to his beliefs. You could have killed him, but you could not get him to compromise his integrity.

I personally don't understand how anyone can look at the world around them with all it's intricate details and interdependencies and come to the conclusion that it all just evolved, or happened by chance, but if that is your conclusion, I'll pray for you. As long as you are still alive there is the possibility that you will one day see the light. I'm afraid that if you don't come to believe in God while you are alive, you won't enjoy meeting him after you die.

I realize that the lessons and the stories I have written are not the most inspiring stories ever written. I also realize that without the personal mentor/protégé relationship that existed between Ralph and myself, that you may not get as much instruction from these lessons as I did. Ralph helped me to identify and define for myself the rules that I strive to live by. However, rules without relationship produce rebellion. He never tried to enforce his rules on me. So I do not propose that you should live your life according to my rules. But I do believe that you should first of all determine the rules that you will live by, and then set about living your life as you have predetermined. Don't leave your future to chance or circumstances.

Ralph taught that the difference between rich people and poor people is primarily in the way that they think. Anyone can do what rich people do; it's just that they don't know what it is that rich people do that makes them wealthy. So Ralph started out by getting me to *think*. Then he set about the task of getting me *thinking right*. We were friends for over ten years, so obviously I can't put everything he ever told me into this book. As I sift through my notes I will continue to write more stories and lessons and post them on my personal page provided by Music City Publishing where you can read them with no charge. Just go to: www.musiccitypublishing.com then click on author biographies, then on Tim Hendricks Personal Page.

I would also like to get some feedback about the book, so please email me with your comments.

My hope is that something that I have written will cause you to stop and THINK, (which most people don't do much of anymore), and that by thinking, you will find ways to improve your life. And I hope that you will be more inspired to chase your dreams than you were before reading this book. Life without a dream is a dull and boring routine at best. Life with a dream that you are not chasing is frustration to the max. Most of all I hope that you will be inspired to search for and find a mentor to help you to accomplish whatever you decide to do with your life.

A good mentor doesn't just tell you what you need to do to succeed; he says, "I've been across the mine field, I know the shortcuts, the pitfalls, and the booby traps. Come follow me and I'll walk you through it step by step."

My last hope for you is that once you have been shown the way across the minefield of life, that you will be willing to become a mentor for others. Be willing to share your knowledge and wisdom with others who are searching.

One of the greatest needs in the world today is for more people to serve as mentors for the generations to come. You have knowledge and experiences that no one else in the world has. I hope that you will share those experiences with others who are willing to listen. There are people out there who are eager to learn. I hope that you will be as good a mentor to them as Ralph was to me.

Tim & Anna backstage with Kim & Robert Kiyosaki

CHAPTER

TWENTY-TWO

During that eighteen month time period while Ralph was going through tremendous suffering I told him that I didn't understand how he could go on every day with a good attitude. He brought out a copy of "Man's Search for Meaning" by Viktor E. Frankl who had survived the Nazi Death Camps in World War Two, and began quoting from it.

"To live is to suffer, to survive is to find meaning in the suffering. If there is a purpose in life at all, there must be a purpose in suffering and in dying. But no man can tell another what this purpose is."

"A man's suffering is similar to the behavior of gas. If a certain quantity of gas is pumped into an empty chamber, it will fill the chamber completely and evenly, no matter how big the chamber is. Thus, suffering completely fills the human soul and conscious mind, no matter whether the suffering is great or little. Therefore the 'size' of human suffering is absolutely relative."

Ralph said, "You have to learn to ignore the suffering and focus on joy, then a very small amount of pleasure can fill your heart and cause great joy. Learn to let joy fill your conscious mind instead of pain and suffering. I can find something to be happy about every day of my life, so I focus on that."

He quoted Frankl again, "Everything can be taken away from a man but one thing: the last of the human freedoms, and that is the ability to choose one's attitude in any given set of circumstances."

Ralph said, "I know that we were all created by God, and that we are spiritual beings, temporarily held captive by a physical body. Whenever one door closes, another one opens. I don't know what is on the other side of the door of death, but I know that my Savior is on the other side of that door, so I'm not afraid to go through it."

I later picked up a copy of Frankl's book and read some quotes, which I believe, would apply to the life of Ralph Autry. "In the final analysis it becomes clear that the sort of person that anyone becomes is the result of an inner decision, and not the result of outside influences alone. Therefore, any man can under any circumstances decide what shall become of him--mentally and spiritually."

I recently read a quote by Martha Washington along the same lines, she said, "I have learned from experience that the greater part of our happiness or misery depends on our dispositions and not on our circumstances."

In trying to deal with Ralph's passing, I read a lot of books and have come to certain conclusions. I have reached these conclusions on my own, after Ralph's passing, so if you do not agree with anything I write in the rest of this chapter, please do not let it be a poor reflection on Ralph, since he was not here for me to run these ideas by, before presenting them.

I believe that the human spirit cannot be defeated or taken away from anyone against his will; it can only be surrendered voluntarily. I believe that a person who has a reason to live can endure almost any amount of pain and suffering. Whether the reason is a loved one here on earth, or an all-consuming passion or mission, or whether it be a spiritual reason such as we find in the suffering of the apostle Paul.

I remember the questions I had in my own mind, "Why am I here? What is the purpose of me going through all this pain and misery just to end up dying?" I finally stopped asking, "What is the meaning of life, or what can I expect from life?" Instead I began to think that I was put here for a purpose; and life, (or maybe the Lord) is continually asking me, "Are you taking on the responsibilities that life has put in your hands right now, today, or, are you avoiding them? Are you fulfilling the tasks that have been set before you? Are you all talk, or do you conduct yourself in a right manner and do what is right? Are you doing what ought to be done, when it ought to be done, whether you like it or not?"

I believe that the meaning of life will be different for every person and it will be different from hour to hour for every person because we all have different tasks and responsibilities to fulfill which are different from every other person. You cannot, and therefore should not, compare your life or your destiny to that of any other person, because you have different situations, different tasks, and different abilities. Sometimes we find ourselves in situations that allow us to shape our own destiny by our actions. At other times, whether it is called accident, fate, or whatever, we will simply have to accept what has happened and deal with it as best we can. As Ralph said, play the cards that have been dealt you. Can we work towards a better life? Certainly. But deal with the life you have right now as best you can. Do what you do with pride and dignity knowing that you are giving it your best.

When Ralph suddenly found out that it was his destiny to suffer with inoperable cancer, he accepted that as his task and his responsibility. He never asked for sympathy or pity; in fact, even from stage, he insisted that no one treat him with sympathy or pity. He knew that no one could relieve him of his suffering, or suffer in his place, it was his task and his alone, and he handled it superbly.

Too many people, I believe, when faced with pain and suffering want to cry, "Why me? It just isn't fair." Some even say, "I can't expect anything more from life," so they decide to just commit suicide and get it over with.

They don't realize that there may be a purpose for their suffering. Something may be expected of them in the future. Their pain and suffering may put them into a unique position of being able to help others who have to go through the same, or similar suffering. Bearing their cross courageously may inspire and give hope to others who are facing difficult times. I believe that there is someone watching every one of us during difficult times. It may be a friend or family member, alive or dead, or maybe even the Lord. They do not expect for us to wimp out and disappoint them. They hope to find us suffering with dignity; not miserably, whining and complaining to everyone around. I think that we should all face the fact that we are all eventually going to die. Some will have to suffer through more than others. When the winds of adversity blow into your life don't let them blow you away. Face into the wind, and like a kite, let that wind take you to new heights, to see things as you have never seen them before, and then share those insights with others, just as Ralph Autry did.

Whatever we individually experience in our lives, no power on earth can ever take from us. Everything we have thought, what we have said or done, and what we have experienced makes us unique in the entire world.

We can choose to throw away that vast amount of knowledge and experience, or we can choose to pass it on for the benefit of others.

We all have a story to tell, and we can all learn something from every other human being who has had different experiences than our own.

I believe that a person who lives his life trying to accumulate everything for himself will be miserable. Whether it is fame or fortune, no matter how much you 'get', it will never be enough.

True joy comes from giving to others. The more you do things to benefit others the more joy you will get for yourself. I dare you to go out and do something nice for someone else with no thought of financial or social reward, and see if the feelings that you get from it don't make it worth the time and effort. In fact, I'd like for you to mail or email me a note and explain what you did and how it made you feel.

I believe that while we are here on earth, we should not worry. Worry causes stress and anxiety, which can cause all manner of illnesses. If you know who you are, why you are here, and where you are going, then there is nothing to worry about. If you don't know any of that, you may want to start figuring it out. I believe that a good place to start is in the Bible. I also believe that you should be careful in your choice of which Bible you read. There are many versions out today which were not translated from the original manuscripts, but were paraphrased by one man, or a few men, or by a particular denomination. In that case, you don't get the inspired word of God. You get the opinions of one man, or just a few men, who have set out to prove to the world that the Bible says what they believe it to say. You get their *opinions* or their *interpretation* of what they *think* the original manuscript meant.

In my opinion, *opinions* are like armpits. Everyone has a couple of them, and most of them stink. Don't base your eternal salvation on another human beings opinion, even mine.

Get a Bible that is a *translation* of the original, not a *transliteration*, or a *paraphrased* version, and study it. The Bible is actually a collection of sixty-six books written by forty different people over a period of fifteen hundred years and contains over six hundred prophecies about one single individual. Every single one of those prophecies was fulfilled by one person named Jesus who can be proven to have lived, through secular records, just as convincingly as they could prove that George Washington lived. I don't believe that all of that could happen without the writers being inspired by a supernatural being.

The Authorized King James version of the Bible is probably the most accurate translation from the original scrolls and letters but many people don't like reading it because of the sixteenth century English wording. The New King James Version was redone in modern English and is very good. I personally prefer the American Standard Version. Just be very careful when you study that you aren't getting some individuals *opinion*.

I believe that every human being has the freedom to choose his course of action at any instant. We may be able to predict the general direction of a group based on statistical analysis or on the bell curve, but the actions or attitude of any individual will remain totally unpredictable. We are all affected by biological, psychological, and social conditions, but we each have the power and capability to ignore the past, ignore conditions, and make a decision to move in a new direction, or to act in a different way.

Every human being has the capacity to do great good, and every human has the capacity to do great evil. Which one we choose depends on our own decisions, not on external circumstances or conditions. The people who accomplish great things on this earth are not the ones who were born with the best talent, or who had the greatest ability, but simply the ones who make a decision to accomplish something great or unusual, and start to work towards it, learn as they go, and never give up.

Therefore, the simple decisions that we make each and every day eventually build the monument to our lives that people will remember us by. So deciding in advance how we would like to be remembered will have, or at least should have, an impact on the decisions that we make each day of our lives.

By setting goals we give our subconscious mind a final destination that we would like to reach. The subconscious mind then sets about to take you to that predetermined destination by the quickest possible route. If you do not have any goals set, the mind has to make decisions instantly, based on whatever facts or evidence is available at the moment to the conscious mind.

Imagine for a moment two young people in Florida who both decide to take a trip. The one sets a goal to go to California. His mind immediately starts looking for the shortest or quickest route, or maybe even a map to take him there. Even if he should get off course, he will keep referring to the map, or if the person is a female she will continually stop and ask directions. (Men would prefer to wander for hours before asking directions.) Eventually the person must attain the goal of reaching California, assuming that the person does not quit along the way. There is no other alternative.

How long the trip takes will depend on many variables, but the outcome is predictable, they arrive in California.

The other person decides to take a trip, but fails to set a definite goal or to pick a destination. They simply start moving. At each crossroads or intersection, they look at the evidence immediately around them and make a decision on which way to go based on how things look in the immediate vicinity, or on how they feel that day. The outcome in this case is also predictable. They will wander around from here to there, and back and forth, and even stopping to ask for directions will be to no avail, simply because they don't know where they want to go and they have never set a goal to get there. They would probably never even get out of Florida. This is how most people live their lives.

Before I met Ralph, my idea of long range planning was lunch. However living by wandering around is not what we were created for. We are by nature goal setting, goal-achieving beings. Anyone who has raised children can attest to this. No one has to teach a child to set a goal to crawl, and then teach him or her how to achieve it. It happens naturally. Then to stand, then to walk, etc. But somewhere along the way, this instinct to set a goal and go after it until we achieve it no matter how long it takes or how difficult it may be is educated out of us. We turn over the goal setting to our parents, or a peer group, or another influence, and we let someone else decide for us what we should be working toward, with the end result that we don't really strive to attain it, because it wasn't our hearts desire to start with.

There are many good books on goal setting and on every other subject that you might want to learn. I highly recommend that you don't stop your education just because you are out of school because that is when life's real lessons start.

I believe that people who have a personal mentor:

1) Who cares for them,
2) That they respect,
3) That they want respect from,
4) Who is guiding them to a better, more successful life,
5) That they can hold themselves accountable to, typically do not get involved in alcohol, drugs, crime, or depression. People get into all those things because they are self-centered, and don't have goals and dreams of a better life. If they had dreams in the past, they have given up any hope they once had of achieving them.

People who are focused on trying to make themselves happy become miserable and turn to depression, alcohol, and drugs to try to escape the nightmare of running the rat race day after day until they die broke. Statistics are all around us that prove that approximately ninety-five percent of all Americans who even reach the age of sixty-five will be broke and dependent on the government, or relatives for their meager existence. One quick look at their financial situation tells people that they are a part of that ninety-five percent, because they know that the minute they quit working the money stops coming in.

Since they don't know what to do about it, and it is too painful to face, they try to act like everything is alright, and then they go out and get drunk or drugged so that they can escape and not have to face it for a while.

I believe that having a mentor who we love and respect that will point out our shortcomings, is the only way that most of us will accept that we need help in a particular area. The value of a mentor cannot be over-rated. Every row is rough to hoe without a friend to cheer you on.

Let's face it; if reading books alone would help us to solve all of our problems, then, all of our problems would have been solved long ago. We have read the books that claimed that they had the answer to our challenges. We have heard the audio recordings and been to the seminars that claimed to be the ultimate solution. I think that what most of us need is a trusted advisor that will gently make us aware that no matter how good we think we are, we still need improvement in certain areas. Then they help us to develop a plan or a strategy of improvement and allow us to hold ourselves accountable to them so that we can measure our improvements and our results.

Let me make it clear that I am not denying that books, audio recordings, and seminars are great tools for accumulating knowledge. I personally believe that they are vital to our personal growth and development and I am a great promoter of them all. I just believe that a personal mentor is the missing ingredient that keeps most of us from realizing our goals and dreams. A mentor pulls all the information together and helps us to apply it to our own lives in ways that we can't do for ourselves. They help us to turn all of that accumulated knowledge into wisdom. We all have blind spots. We can't see ourselves objectively, as others can. Therefore a mentor who has our best interest at heart should be a vital part of our success strategy. Close association with someone who refuses to compromise with circumstances he does not like, is an asset whose value can never be measured in terms of money. A mentor can give acceptance and a sense of belonging that all of us need.

I have had people point out to me that success isn't everything. Success isn't everything but it allows a man to stand straight and hold his head up.

If you can identify your purpose in life, that will help you to decide which fork in the road to take every day of your life. The decision making process becomes much easier when you know the final destination that you want to reach. Once you have identified, or chosen that purpose or mission and set some definite goals, written them down so that you can review them regularly, start working on developing a more positive attitude. What you actually achieve in life will be determined by the talent or skill that you have, or that you are capable of developing. What you attempt to do will be determined by your hopes and dreams and the amount of motivation behind them. Your attitude is the determining factor in whether you will achieve all that you are capable of, or whether you will fall short. We all have challenges, adversities, and problems that we face in life. A person with a poor attitude runs into obstacles and quits, or makes excuses about why he or she can't move on, and starts looking for someone else to blame for their failure. A person with a good attitude realizes that all winners or achievers faced obstacles that seemed to be insurmountable, but they endured, they pressed on, they sought out ways to go over, under, around the obstacle, or they just kept getting better themselves, until the obstacle was no longer insurmountable to them.

Ralph taught that you couldn't build a business, a reputation, or anything else on what you intend to do. You have to begin. You have to get out of the stands and onto the playing field. The way that we grow stronger is not by avoiding resistance, but by pressing against it until we develop more strength. It is a proven fact that you don't become a better athlete by continually playing against people less skilled than yourself, but by going up against people who are better than you are. Which means that you will be defeated time after time. But while you are going through that process of losing in the short term, you are actually winning, because your skills will improve as a result of competing with someone more skilled than yourself.

I know an individual who has only been beaten once in his entire life in one-on-one basketball. You may think that it is one of the all time great basketball players. I can assure you that every great basketball player, or any other great player in any other sport for that matter, has been beaten many, many times. The guy who has only been beaten one time played his first game of one-on-one when he was ten years old and someone who had been playing for a while beat him. He has never been beaten since, simply because he has never played basketball again in his life. We don't become superstars or achievers by avoiding losing; we become winners by losing and learning. If you lose and learn long enough, you begin to win.

So develop the attitude that you will win in the long run, even if you do suffer setbacks along the way. I remember reading a story about one of the greatest heavyweight boxers that ever lived. He got knocked down on the canvas over and over, every fight that he entered, and yet he became the heavyweight champion of the world. When asked how he had achieved that title even though he got knocked down so many times, he responded, "I always get back up one more time than I get knocked down." His attitude said that it didn't matter to him how he did in the short term, what mattered to him was to be the only man standing when the final bell rang.

Many times in life we can become the lead figure in our field just by remaining strong and standing firm while the competition falls away. Ralph called it, "S.I.E." Self Inflicted Elimination. Many people, who have greater intelligence, more innate ability, and perhaps even superior skill, will not be around long term due to self-inflicted elimination. They don't have a positive, can-do, attitude, and so they quit, when they could have become champions.

I personally worked long and hard until I was in my early thirties only to achieve a negative net worth of about fifty thousand dollars. I had over fifty thousand dollars in consumer debt, no home, less than two hundred dollars in my checking account, no savings, and no investments. Within five years of finding a mentor, I was able to pay off all the debt, purchase a nice home, and create substantial savings and investments.

Try this plan to change your future. Spend five percent of your time every day doing something that will change your future. There are one thousand four hundred and forty minutes in a day. Five percent of that will be seventy-two minutes. Even if you spend ninety five percent of every day putting out fires and taking care of daily chores, if you will just spend five percent of your time daily educating yourself about financial matters, business opportunities, relationships, skills that will help you such as people skills, leadership skills, time management skills, etc. and then spend that time taking action to make something happen, in just a few years, your circumstances can change dramatically. Is five percent of your time too much to ask, on a regular basis, to become the kind of person you dream of being?

One of my favorite quotes is from 'Old Hickory' Andrew Jackson, who said, "One man with courage makes a majority."

I believe that one man or woman who is committed will out-perform ten who are only interested.

You can have an impact on the world. You can make a difference. But you need a mentor to help you to get started and to keep you headed in the right direction. Find one. Accomplish something unusual so that the world will take notice. Then, when you open your mouth to share your beliefs and ideas, they will have a reason to listen.

When you have a personal mentor who has a personal interest in you, you don't just get the general success principles that you can read in any of hundreds of different books. You get personalized advice, one-on-one coaching and training, and you get a relationship that no book, no course, or seminar can give you. There are things a mentor can do that no book or recording can do. A mentor can love you, comfort you, console you, touch you, forgive you and help you to forgive yourself, edify and build you up to yourself and to others. A mentor can help you do what you have set out to do, work with you and show you how to do things in a better more efficient way.

A mentor can make you aware of your shortcomings and how to overcome them. Ralph taught in this manner:

I do you watch.

I do you help.

You do I help.

You do I watch.

You do I coach.

No book in the world can do that. Too many people I fear have fallen into the trap of believing that they can just read a book, listen to a recording, or go to a seminar, and then go out into the world and apply all that information effectively and be successful. A few can, but I believe that most of us need a mentor who can open for us windows number three and four. Forgive me for not remembering the details of who developed it, or the exact description of the 'four windows' but I'll explain it as well as I can remember.

Window number one contains things that I know about myself that you can also know about me from seeing me, or meeting me. For example, we may both know the color of my skin and hair, how tall or short I am, etc.

Window number two contains things that I know about myself that no one else in the world knows. Things that I have done when I was alone that I have never told anyone, or things that I have thought and never expressed, would be in this window.

Window number three contains things that you know about me that I do not know. You may be aware of the fact that I have bad breath, whereas I don't have a clue. You may notice that I have a continuous twitch that I am not aware of. You may know that I have the potential to achieve great things in a particular field, and I don't have the slightest idea that I even have any potential.

Window number four contains things that I don't know about myself and you don't know about me. When the 'experts' told Elvis not to give up his truck-driving job because he would never make it as a singer, neither Elvis nor the others had any clue of the potential that he held as an entertainer. When Michael Jordan got kicked off his high school basketball team I don't believe that he or the coach had any idea that he could become one of the greatest players to ever play the game.

What a mentor can do is to make us aware of things in window number three that will help us, and a mentor can also help us to discover and develop things contained in window number four that we may never have become aware of on our own. Colonel Tom Parker took Elvis under his wing and exposed Elvis' window number four to himself and to the world.

Let's say that you wanted to learn to play basketball good enough to become a professional. Would you rather read some books about how to play and then get out there in your driveway to start learning from experience, or, would you rather go to the local YMCA basketball clinic, or, would you rather spend several hours a week on the court, one-on-one, with Michael Jordan? (Or any other top NBA player who had a personal interest and who wanted to see you succeed).

Using the basketball analogy the value of a mentor becomes obvious. However, most people don't see the value of a mentor in business or in life, but the same value is there.

Could you become a better actor by reading a book, or by studying one-on-one with Sean Connery and becoming his protégé?

Would you become a great magician by reading a book, joining a local magic club, or by becoming David Copperfield's protégé?

Imagine the impact on the world if everyone who achieved greatness in any field would mentor at least five or six others and help them to achieve their dreams and accomplish more than they ever could have without a mentor's guidance. If those six would then share their knowledge, experience, and wisdom with six others and teach them to do the same thing, imagine the possibilities.

I suggest that you find a mentor, identify your dreams, make a commitment to spending your life chasing your dreams, (not being a couch potato watching actors, entertainers, and athletes pursuing their dreams), develop a plan, take action, and have a great life. Then become a mentor for others and teach them to do the same thing, and together we can change this world for the better, just as Ralph Autry did.

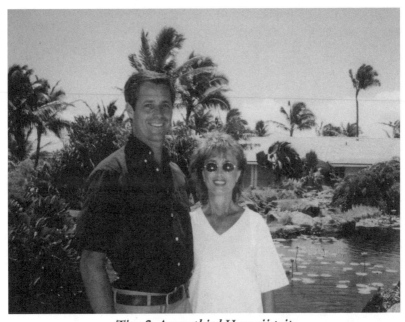

Tim & Anna third Hawaii trip

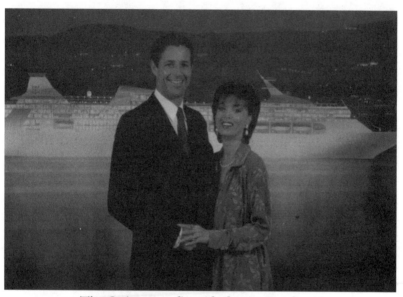

Tim & Anna on first Alaska Cruise aboard
Royal Caribbean's Rhapsody of the Seas

Tim boarding float plane for
Taku Glacier Lodge Juneau Alaska

*Tim, Anna, Betty, and friends at Gaylord's Plantation
our favorite Hawaiian restaurant on Kauai*

*Tim and his dad fly fishing Yellowstone River
in Northwest Wyoming.*

TWENTY-THREE

After writing the first twenty-two chapters of this book, I thought that it was finished. Then I went back and read it through from start to finish and even though it contains a lot of stories and lessons, which, I believe, will help the people who will implement those lessons into their lives, it just didn't seem to be complete. It did not really express my true feelings for my mentor, nor did it express the depth of character or the strong beliefs that Ralph had, which I wanted to portray. So, knowing that my lack of education in the English language was hindering me from expressing my deep feelings, and realizing that I didn't know the words with which to express myself, I determined to do as Ralph had taught me to do, which is to study a topic until I could comprehend it and apply it to my life. I decided to read and study to find the words that I didn't use in everyday life that would most accurately describe the true character of Ralph Autry. From this point forward, you may get the idea that the words and phrases you read are not words that you would hear coming from the mouth of a lifelong blue collar worker, and you will be correct. They have not yet become a part of my everyday vocabulary, but with continued use, perhaps they will.

Let me begin with a more accurate description of the man I knew as Ralph Autry. Then I wish to make a few observations of my own. I now believe that Ralph was actually the sum total of the spirit of many men whom he had chosen to imitate and emulate. They may have been dead for many years, yet their spirit and influence lived on through his life and through his influence. Observing the life of Ralph Autry gave me a clearer image of who I wanted to be.

Ralph was never ashamed of humble origins. He was not born into wealth or fame and believed that any man could do what any other man had done. He devoted himself to study, regarded time as a treasure that was limited, and determined to make the best use of it. He was very conscientious and always studied in depth any subject that he was to speak about so that he could give the listener his best thoughts, expressed in the very best manner, and most easily understood by them. He never tired of improving himself and his talks to the point that very little, if any fault could be found in his words. His success as a speaker was the result of painstaking labor and diligent effort.

He was of the opinion that it was good to spend at least a small portion of every day working in what would be called an occupation. Having been a Pharmacist, who no longer needed to work in that field to support himself, he continued to stay current in that field, believing that work was good for stimulating the higher faculties.

It was not by luck or accident that Ralph achieved distinction, but rather by sheer persistence and hard work. Though he achieved wealth, this was not his primary motive. In fact, the mere love of money could never have sustained the continual efforts that he and Betty put forth year after year. Their pleasure was in pursuing their purpose of making a difference in other people's lives, their best rewards, seeing the difference they had made; the wealth which followed being only incidental.

Napoleon Bonaparte who stood five feet two inches tall and weighed one hundred and thirty pounds said, "A leader is a dealer in hope." Whether you approve of Napoleons politics or not, one must admit that he was a leader. By his definition, Ralph was very much a leader. People were attracted to him and enjoyed being around him because he gave them hope. Hope of becoming more of the person they wanted to be, hope of greater recognition for their efforts, and hope of a better life both here on this earth and in the life to come.

Ralph was a man of perpetual activity and was always on the move. He claimed to have gasoline in his veins and was always ready to set out on a new adventure. One of his favorite sayings was, "No talk, just action, watch my smoke."

He was careful to take advantage of all opportunities for improvement that came his way. He had diligently studied the methods and the beliefs of the best in his chosen field of business and practiced until he had mastered the basics and the principles that had taken them to the top.

Ralph never despised the long hours and the drudgery of counting pills that he had endured to support his family early in his career. He believed that it did him good, familiarizing him with steady work, and cultivating in him the spirit of patience and the discipline that would later help him to build a worldwide business empire.

Early in his business career he was told by someone who was very well known and highly respected in his own business field, different from Ralph's industry, that in order to excel he would have to focus his whole mind upon his business from the time he arose until he went to bed, and that being married would hinder him from ever achieving greatness, and that regularly attending worship services of the church would keep him from achieving anything substantial. Ralph and Betty proved him wrong on both counts, achieving great success in the business world, without affecting their priorities of spiritual matters first, family matters second, and business worked into the fabric of their lives; as opposed to work being first priority and family and spiritual matters being worked in (or forgotten) as we see in too many business leaders in the world today.

Having been a continual vexation to Ralph, I can personally attest to the fact that his patience seemed absolutely inexhaustible. Though he was a man of powerful individuality, he displayed great restraint and genuine concern for those who were not as strong of character. He left behind an enduring reputation of pure and high-minded intent, fortitude that seemed inexhaustible, and great character untarnished by avarice or low passion. A man of dauntless will, prompt, vigorous, and daring, and yet he displayed a great amount of generosity.

He had formed in his mind, while still a young man, the romantic vision of building a business empire, while working out of his home, which would be a residual source of income. This would give him the freedom to be a full time husband to his wife and father to his children and would also give him the time that he wanted to devote to the church and to helping others to have a better life. The dream became a passion that he pursued throughout his life with determination and calm but indomitable force of will which were but a few of the attributes of his character.

The man had extraordinary courage and determination. When difficulties surrounded him and threatened to destroy his resolve they only succeeded in making him dig in that much deeper. His determined energy and cool courage set an excellent example for others to follow. I never heard him utter a word of despair and I am confident that he would never have considered surrender under any circumstances. His faith and devotion to God would give him ultimate triumph regardless of his earthly fate. He gave honor to the human race. He may have belonged to the same group of ordinary people whom we meet daily on the streets; but when disaster fell upon him, he displayed a wealth of personal resources and energy, and became, in my opinion, individually heroic.

Borne up by invincible courage and never-failing patience, he worked in a spirit of sublime self-sacrifice, without any thought of worldly honor, inspired solely by the hope of seeking out and rescuing the lost and fallen souls he saw all around him. When he could have been sitting at home in comfort and ease, he was often found traveling the roads late into the night, sometimes not getting home until the sun was coming up. He was willing to inconvenience himself to the extreme in order to set an example for others, such as myself, to follow knowing that our current educational system had for the most part eliminated the teaching of any moral values, godly principles, or character building traits. He proved by his life that there are higher objectives in the world than social status, and nobler aspirations than the accumulation of wealth. He was a true gentleman in speech as well as in actions; brave, honorable, generous; easily led by his mentors, yet perfectly capable of leading; able to be persuaded if the facts were provable, yet himself very persuasive in his own beliefs.

The life of Ralph Autry backed up his teaching that whatever you do should be done well. He said that it was better to accomplish a small amount of work perfectly, or at least well, than to half-do ten times as much. His magnificent business qualities were felt around the globe, and there can be no doubt that, by the care with which he provided for every contingency, and the personal attention that he gave to every detail, he laid the foundations of his own success. Integrity, in word and deed, was the very cornerstone of all his business transactions. He found not only honor and reputation, but also substantial success, in always delivering what he promised, and in always having things turn out to be what he represented them to be.

Having been in business now for some years myself, I can attest to the fact that business will try a man's character perhaps more severely than any other pursuit in life. It puts to the severest tests honesty, self-denial, justice, truthfulness, and integrity; and men of business who pass through such trials unstained are perhaps worthy of as great honor as soldiers who prove their courage amidst the fire and dangers of the battlefield. Surrounded by all of the temptations to which wealth gives access, Ralph proved himself beyond reproach. It may be that the totally honest man may not grow rich as fast as the unscrupulous and dishonest one; but his success will be of a truer kind, earned without fraud or injustice. Even though a man should be less successful for a time, I believe that he should still be honest. I think it would be better to lose all financially and keep a good character, than to gain financially and lose credibility and reputation. Character itself is worth a fortune, and if a man will hold to his principles, success will eventually come his way, both here in this world, as Ralph proved, and in the world to come. Very few men stand the test of success as well as Ralph handled it.

Ralph had the power to resist instant gratification for the purpose of securing a future good for his family, which is something we rarely see in this day and time of an instant gratification society; with fast food, credit card buy now-pay later plans, and a general striving to keep up with the neighbors lifestyle. He let mental reasoning take control over animal instincts. He did not make money, or the things it could buy, his idol, but regarded money as a useful tool, which could accomplish much good when put into the right hands with right plans. He considered the ambition to dazzle others with the appearance of worldly success a total waste of time and money. That was the kind of thing done by miserable folks, which usually led to bankruptcy. He believed that the discipline would be always found most valuable which is acquired by resisting small present gratifications to secure a prospective greater and higher one.

I found a picture of a banner above a broken helmet in Battle Abbey (Founded in 1067 by William the Conqueror, to commemorate his victory at Senlac which gave him control of England). On the banner was a motto that said, 'There is, indeed, no blessing equal to the possession of a stout heart. Even if a man fails in his efforts, it will be a satisfaction to him to enjoy the consciousness of having done his best. In humble life nothing can be more cheering and beautiful than to see a man combating suffering by patience, triumphing in his integrity, and who, when his feet are bleeding and his limbs failing him, still walks upon his courage.'

Ralph's entire life presented a striking example of a stout heart, triumphing through integrity, walking upon his courage, perseverance, diligence, self-culture, continual self-improvement and increasing knowledge, and untiring devotion to his Lord and to his family.

Ralph left a legacy to his children and to the world of a life well spent, a character uprightly sustained, courage under extreme adversity, truthfulness, integrity, goodness, strength of purpose, and generosity seldom seen.

Disraeli said, "The youth who does not look up will look down; and the spirit that does not soar is destined perhaps to grovel."

Ralph was a great example of a spirit that soared, and the wonderful influence he had on so many lives will continue to be felt throughout generations to come.

A man once said, "There is no action of man in this life, which is not the beginning of so long a chain of consequences, as that no human providence is high enough to give us a prospect to the end."

Another quote I found said, "Our youth owe more of their education to the lives which they read and the examples which they witness than to the instruction which they receive." We should all be very careful about what our children read, how we live our lives in front of them, and who we show admiration for in the presence of our children, because chances are, they will strive to grow up to be like those people.

One man said, "The worth of a State, in the long run, is the worth of the individuals composing it."

Ralph knew that example teaches without words and that example is one of the most potent of instructors. It is the real world of teaching by action and is much more forceful than words. Good advice has its place, but if it is not accompanied by a good example it will carry very little influence. We often hear people say, "Do as I say, not as I do," but in the vast majority of cases, they do exactly as you do, regardless of what you say. Let him first be a man, then it matters not what his status or occupation may be, he will be a good example to those about him.

What is seen through the eye makes a far deeper impression on human beings than what is heard or read. This is especially true in the early years when the eye is the primary inlet of knowledge, since babies do not understand our language. Whatever children see they will unconsciously imitate. They will automatically come to resemble those with whom they spend the most time. It has been said that by the age of six years old, a persons general attitudes toward life have already been instilled, and the people they have spent most of their waking hours with have instilled them. So I believe as Ralph did that our homes should be the primary training ground for the future generations so that we can form the character that will determine their actions for the rest of their lives. The home is a mirror of future society, the birthplace of national character, whether it be pure or tainted. The primary influence on tens of thousands of children being raised today is television. The only heroes today's children know are actors, entertainers, and athletes. If these people exhibit the characteristics and morals that we would have our children to duplicate then all is well. However, too often we find just the opposite. A person's success in the field of acting, entertaining, or athletics all too often has little or nothing whatsoever to do with good character, decent morals, or virtue. They are very good in their chosen field of endeavor, and once having attained success, they are held up as symbols of what our young people should strive to be like in every area of life, not just in that career. We have simply to look at the many, many news stories that have come out over the years concerning these 'heroes' to see what our young will be imitating: lying, cheating, stealing, spousal abuse, drug addiction, drug dealing, alcoholism, sexual immorality, tax fraud and on and on. I understand that the Constitution gives us freedom of speech so that because of success in his or her field a mere actor, entertainer, or athlete can go on television and express his personal views about religion or politics in front of a national audience. But I wish that someone could explain to me what twisted and perverted train of thought could possibly possess anyone to think that those folk's opinions, outside their field of knowledge, have any value or merit whatsoever, if not based on facts.

The habits, morals, and principles taught in the home today will be the way our nation is governed in the future. When I look at how the majority of children are being raised, and I look at the utter lack of morals, good habits, and character that children living today are being raised with, I shutter to think of what our nation must go through in coming years. My hope is that you, the reader, will strive to be a good example even in seemingly trivial matters, because our influence is constantly being inter-woven into the fabric of the lives of others, and contributing to form their character, for better or for worse.

I believe that the best thing that we can do to improve our children's lives, and thereby improve our nation, is to improve ourselves. As our morals improve, so will our children's, and our nation's.

When I first read the line quoted previously about every action we take beginning a long line of consequences, it hit me like a physical blow. The thought that there is not an act done or a word uttered by a human being that does not carry with it a train of consequences, the end of which we will never know, is both wonderful, and scary. Every good deed we do will send out ripples, like a pebble tossed into a pond, which will impact many people over time. But every misdeed, violent act, bad attitude, or poor example will also create a ripple effect with compounding negative results. The poor attitude of a father toward a race of people, even though the father remains insignificant on the stage of the world, can influence a child to grow up to be Adolf Hitler.

The positive influence of a loving mother telling her child that he will one day accomplish something great for the good of the world can cause a child to grow up to be Five Star General Douglas Macarthur who believed his mother had been talking about that precise moment in time, and so he returned to the Philippines in World War Two to free that nation from the forces which occupied the country.

Throughout history we can see that the spirits of men and women do not die; they still live and walk abroad among us. No person is so insignificant as to be sure that his example will not do a great amount of good, or a great amount of evil through the lives of others.

As the events of today are rooted in the past, and the lives and examples of our ancestors still influence us, so we are, by our daily actions contributing to form the character of future generations. Our daily actions, attitudes, and words will echo throughout eternity, influencing those yet to be born.

Though our bodies return to the dust, our good or bad deeds will still be bearing fruit after their kind for many years to come. This places a great responsibility upon us both individually and as a nation, and is something that we should not take lightly.

Ralph and I had numerous conversations over the years concerning America's educational system, values, morals, and the fate of nations who abandoned Godly principles. Having been raised in a good home with God fearing and God loving parents, his beliefs and his teaching confirmed what I believed and helped me to solidify my thinking. I believe that there were principles put into place at the foundation of the world, which, when we work in cooperation with them, our lives generally go much smoother. When we try to live our lives in violation of these basic laws, or principles, life gets very hard. Show me a person who is having an extremely difficult time, and I will show you a person who is trying to live in violation of at least one basic law, and probably more than one.

Because of Ralph's influence, I believe that the best method of education in terms of character comes from models. We unconsciously mold ourselves after the people with whom we spend the most time. When it comes to manners, habits, opinions, and character, good rules may help, but good models will help far more. Realizing this, we should take great care in determining and consciously deciding with whom we will spend the most of our time. We should also take a close interest in who our children are spending most of their time around, knowing that they will, without the least intent of doing so, become more and more like those people. Throughout history we see examples of heroic deeds performed by ordinary men because of the outstanding leadership by which they were inspired. Reading the stories of these heroes or seeing films about their deeds stirs men's blood and makes us strive for greatness in our own lives.

We would do well to read the biographies of great men and women of the past for these would serve as noble models for us to deliberately form the character that we would like to leave to posterity. A book containing the life and deeds of a good and just man is full of precious seed that may bring new life to people in generations to come. The famous poet John Milton wrote of a biography, "It is the precious life-blood of a master-spirit, embalmed and treasured up on purpose to a life beyond life."

That type of book never ceases to exert an uplifting and ennobling influence on its readers.

Benjamin Franklin, in his autobiography attributed his usefulness and eminence to his having read Cotton Mather's 'Essays to do Good', a book about Mather's own life. Many men have said that they framed their own lives, after the model left by Benjamin Franklin in his writings. I believe that it would be much to our society's advantage to keep our citizens reading the best books, so that they can wisely admire and imitate the best characteristics that we find in them.

The noblest possession a man can claim is a good character. With it he may walk with dignity regardless of his station or status in society. It will secure honor and influence and command the general confidence and respect of mankind. Men of character are the conscience of society.

The civilization of nations, as well as their strength depends upon individual character, and the foundations of a civil society rest upon it. Godly people seeking to escape the tyranny of evil and oppressive governments founded the United States of America. The country prospered and was blessed because of the founders stand for truth and justice.

From my study of history there seems to be a continual pattern, or cycle that the world goes through, over and over. God-fearing men decide to fight against that which is evil and corrupt, and eventually take control. They pass laws based on a standard and establish peace and tranquility. There being no wars to fight, the next few succeeding generations begin to turn more and more to individual pleasures, and slowly but surely, individually and as a nation they become fat, lazy, apathetic, undisciplined, and give themselves totally over to indulgences. Then evil rises up to take control. Evil never rests and when good men are not continually on watch, it will creep back in. Good people see what is beginning to happen but don't want to give up their peace and serenity to once again enter the fray. So evil continues to spread its influence until the day when it can take total control of a school, a church, an institution, and eventually the entire nation. Then good people are harassed, persecuted, executed, and driven out, and the land is given totally over to wickedness and indulgences of every type.

Either man will choose to be governed by God and his word, and live peaceful lives in a civilized society, or by rejecting God they choose to be governed by tyrants who will murder, rob, rape, and pillage them, their families, and the country.

The mighty Roman empire with it's unstoppable armies, once having achieved its goal of conquering the world, finally relaxed and began to enjoy the victory. Having no military heroes to hold up as examples to the young, they developed the gladiator arena. Hundreds of thousands would slave away at their assigned duties until the weekend when they could come together for a huge drunken party to watch their favorite warriors beat on one another. History tells us that it is not long after this point in the cycle, when the most important thing on the minds of the majority of people is entertainment and sport, that a country will begin to unravel and fall apart from within.

When I see news coverage of only twenty people gathering to welcome home the American soldiers who have been overseas fighting deadly battles in order to keep our country free from terrorists, and then I see hundreds of millions gathering in cities all over America to party and watch the annual clash of the final two teams in the ultimate showdown of modern gladiators, I wonder if the cycle must repeat itself, or if there is any way to stop it. Please don't get me wrong. I find nothing inherently wrong with sports, entertainment, or having fun. What concerns me is that this seems to be the total focus and the most important thing in so many people's lives.

It happened to the French and the English and it is happening here in America. Having achieved dominance, they relaxed to enjoy the peace. The children and grandchildren of fighters grow up wanting peace and comfort. They never grasp the concept that freedom isn't free because evil never rests. They get into positions of power by promising the voters a free ride; tax the rich and give to the poor, welfare, entitlements, better jobs, higher pay with less work, etc. and once in office it isn't long before the mighty military is reduced to a sideshow. Meanwhile, the Communist apparatus runs true to form. It does not change with time. Communists and Socialists work continually to put themselves in power and are forever eroding the strength of the military services. They know that a free society is ripe for infiltration, and once infiltrated the changes continue in tiny increments until that society is remade into a completely different image. Already there is very little similarity between the country created by The Constitution of the United States of America, and the country we live in today. The vast majority of people in power are so self-serving they refuse to do that which is in the best interest of our nation.

When character is not found in our elected officials we will see a deterioration of morals, a general disregard for laws, and a total lack of respect for decency spread across our land. If we demand no character and no morals of ourselves, we will demand no integrity or character of our leaders. Then judges will rewrite the constitutional laws with their judgments based on their individual opinions, and laws will be passed based on individual legislators opinions or on whichever group promoting their evil ways can come up with the most money to purchase the votes of the self serving officials. As the pendulum swings further away from truth and righteousness people of integrity and character will be proclaimed to be uncaring, discriminating, and intolerant of others. (In reality the godless people screaming "Intolerance!" are in fact the most intolerant group of people on the planet when it comes to accepting other peoples lifestyles and beliefs. They do not want to accept people living by Godly principles, but they insist that we accept them and their godless beliefs!) The whole precept of 'political correctness' is that we must cave in to the Godless and accept their ignorant ranting and disgusting opinions, while at the same time never expressing our Godly views because they might be offended by our views.

I for one am very offended by their language, their views, and their sinful 'lifestyle', which there are laws against, but those laws based on the Constitution are not being enforced because the people in power are afraid to stand up for what is right, because it may cause them to lose the next election. They would rather cave in to evil and remain in power than to do what they were put into power to do.

As more people cave in to their persistent and continuous attacks, evil will not be called evil for fear of offending someone, and despicable sins will be called preference, alternative lifestyle, and artistic expression. After all, the spin-doctors tell us, we should not give preference to one group or another; we should not condemn people for having a different 'lifestyle' than we do, and no one should stop artistic expression, right? (If you agree, you haven't studied the Bible or the United States Constitution)

I believe that what decent people object to, is mislabeling all manner of sin and evil, and inappropriately putting these things into the categories of 'lifestyle' and 'artistic expression' so that the people participating can get by with blatantly breaking the laws that helped to make this a great country. Once they are free to break the law, they set about to change the laws so that the lawbreakers will be protected from the 'intolerant' (people who believe in God and the Constitution). As the cycle continues we will be forced by law to accept sin, evil, and all manner of disgusting activities on the grounds of 'non-discrimination' and 'tolerance'. In the end, individuals, races, and nations will get what they deserve. If good men don't stand up continually for what is right, and base that rightness on an absolute standard, chaos will ensue, and a nation will fall from within. Then the dictators take over and start killing every one who doesn't believe as they do. A quick study of history will show this to be the pattern, over and over, like an unending cycle, until the pendulum swings far enough that good men once again are forced to stand up and fight for their lives, and for what is right, and by force, eliminate the evil from positions of power and reestablish justice and decency through laws based upon a standard. If good men fail to stand up and fight with whatever weapons they have access to, whether for political or religious beliefs, they face extermination from the face of the earth. For this is the ultimate goal of evil. Whether it be a nation or an individual, eventually, if you don't fight for what you believe, your spirit is broken, and you become a slave to those who are willing to fight.

Nation after nation has gone through this cycle and it appears that our country is headed in the same direction. It is a shame that as a nation we can't see what is happening and short circuit the cycle in the middle of its downhill slide and turn the country back to God. But that would mean that we would each individually have to hold ourselves to a higher moral standard than what is currently acceptable. We would then have to leave the comfort of our homes, make a stand for that which is right, with all the reprisals that would then come our way, and possibly give up our lives of endless entertainment and pleasure; all this so that our children or our grandchildren could live in a free society instead of being slaves to a wicked and evil government bureaucracy or a dictator. Again, we will either serve God, or our children will serve tyrant dictators.

In the end, I believe as Ralph did, that God's Will shall prevail, and the righteous shall inherit eternal life in heaven. But I would also like to see a country handed down to our grandchildren with all of the freedoms intact that we have enjoyed in our lives.

Let each one of us therefore strive to live our lives in such a way as to leave a legacy to future generations of honesty, integrity, godliness, goodness, mercy, and justice, just as did my mentor, Ralph Autry.

*I*f you totally disagree with my personal observations of the last few pages I hope that you will forgive me for including them, but these observations were based on conversations I had with Ralph over the years, and I believe that they would also fairly accurately reflect his opinions on these subjects.

*C*arlyle said, "If a book comes from the heart, it will contrive to reach other hearts; all art and authorcraft are of small amount to that."

This book came from my heart and I sincerely hope that something that you have read has reached your heart and that it will help you to become the person you want to become.

Tim & Anna on stage just like Ralph said

Tim Hiking the Colorado Rocky Mountains

⌐⌐ • CHAPTER • ⌐⌐

TWENTY-FOUR

.....The countryside going past the window had transitioned into a city. Our host brought me back into the present by announcing, "Here we are." We had arrived backstage at the auditorium, and the limo door was being opened for us. We entered the building and were greeted by friends that we had come to know and love over the years. We could hear the opening announcements being done as we made our way to the stairway and up to the edge of the stage. I tried to get the butterflies in my stomach to at least fly in formation as we waited just behind the curtain while we were being introduced. Having been a lifelong introvert and an extreme loner, public speaking was not one of my favorite activities.

We had been invited here to tell the story of how we had achieved financial freedom in less than five years. It always amazed me the number of people who were searching for a better life that were willing to come out and listen to us. We knew that there was nothing magical about our achievements. We had simply been willing to work very hard, persistently and consistently, willing to change and grow personally, and willing to follow the pattern and take the suggestions that our mentors had shared with us, until we had replaced my job and her self-employed income with a residual income. We don't view ourselves as big successes, or high achievers. There are many people who have achieved much more than we have. I would also like to point out that when I say that we were financially free, I do not mean that we were rich. Financial freedom, to me, simply meant having enough money coming in from a residual source that neither my wife nor myself had to work a job, and we could continue to live our current lifestyle and have enough money to pay all the bills. There is a big difference to me in financial freedom and being rich. I would define rich as having a million dollars a year in residual income coming in. By that standard, we are not even close to being rich in terms of money. However, I personally have always considered myself to be rich as long as I had good health. It's just that I always wanted to be healthy *and* financially free to live as I chose, instead of being healthy and broke, and having to slave away at a job that I hated just to pay for a roof over my head and mediocre food to eat.

Based on the gentleman's introduction, you would have thought that someone was about to come on stage who was famous, or who had done something great. He finally finished and brought us up, "....please welcome Tim and Anna Hendricks"

We stepped out onto the stage and into the spotlight with the crowd cheering, just like Ralph had said it would happen, many years ago. They didn't know it was just Anna and I; a former hairdresser and a frustrated factory worker who had simply refused to believe that 'you can't change your destiny'.

"Thank you. We are very humbled to be here. We want you to know that we are nothing special and that we haven't done anything that you can't do, in fact, we wouldn't be here at all if it hadn't been for Ralph and Betty Autry. This evening we want to share our story with you, and let you know where we came from and how we got to the position in life where we are now, in the hope that you too will decide to spend your life chasing your dreams. It all started when I found a mentor...."

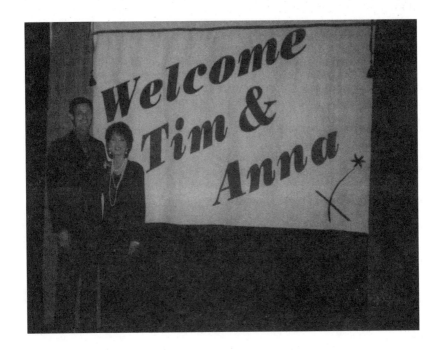

ENDNOTE FROM THE AUTHOR

Since I have never had a class on writing, I would love to have some feedback from the readers of this book, about what you liked or disliked about the book. So please take a moment to write or email me with comments or questions. I'd love to hear from you.

Also, I am continuing my study of the mentor / protégé relationship. If you have a story about a mentor that you would like to share with the world, please send it to me with your permission to include it in a future book about mentors. Anything from one paragraph to a few pages will be considered.

You can send your story, feedback, or any other personal correspondence to me at:

Tim Hendricks
C/O Music City Publishing
P.O. Box 41696
Nashville, Tn. 37204-1696

Or you can email it to:
timhendricks@musiccitypublishing.com

And please remember what Ralph said, "If you are not chasing your dreams, you're not really living, you're just existing."

For years people have been asking me what I currently do for a living. What is my job, career, or profession? The answer is that I do for others what Ralph did for me. I mentor individuals to help them to become successful entrepreneurs. I educate them as to why they should own their own business, then I teach them how to go about getting started, then I coach them until they become profitable. I couldn't find a word in the English language that accurately described what I do, or what I am, so I invented a new word to describe it. *'Entreprementor'*.

My Definition:

Entreprementor;

1) A person who serves as a mentor for aspiring entrepreneurs.
2) An individual who teaches others how to go into business for themselves.

When I first started teaching others to do what I had done, I agreed to work with anyone who expressed an interest. A lot of people wasted a lot of my time. Today, I only work with people who are serious about their financial future, who are teachable, and who prove it by taking action on my suggestions.

I also have a lot of people ask me what I did, or what kind of business I built to gain financial independence. I hesitate to tell them because if they don't have the same education, experiences, background, and access to a good mentor that I had, they may not be able to do exactly what I did. There are many pathways to wealth. Each of us must find our own path. If there was one path that everyone could take successfully to become wealthy, there would only be the need for one 'how to get rich' book on the market. Currently there are hundreds of 'how to get rich' books on the bookstore shelves written by hundreds of people who became wealthy in totally different ways. Many people have read dozens of them and are still broke. I believe that it's not the fault of the books, but simply the fact that not everyone can follow the exact pattern that is written about by another.

That is why I believe that a mentor is so critical. With the book in hand, and a mentor available to develop a relationship with, I believe that a lot more people would be successful. I really believe that the missing ingredient in most people's success formula is the mentor. It may be because they have never found one, or it may be because they refuse to allow anyone to get close enough to them and really understand them to be able to effectively counsel them personally. For me, finding a mentor was the most important and vital ingredient of all, even though I didn't realize it for several years.

I will be writing several chapters that I was not able to include in the book, including chapters on personal responsibility, self-image, leadership, and also a unique story that Ralph told that helped me to understand that deep down burn that made me feel like a caged animal. He said that every creature on earth has an inborn or innate desire to be free. This story had a dramatic impact on my life.

To read these stories and more, go online to
www.musiccitypublishing.com

and click on: Author biographies and Personal Pages
then click on: Tim Hendricks Personal Page
then click on: The Mentor Additional Stories.

Also on my personal page you will find many more pictures of the Autry's and of ourselves, and the lifestyle, which they helped us to create.

ABOUT THE AUTHOR

*T*im considers himself very lucky to have grown up with a great family. His parents have been married for over forty-eight years. His father is a gospel preacher, his mother focused on fulfilling her duties as a wife while raising four children. His mother taught him to admire his father for his integrity, his character, and his love of the Lord. His father taught him to admire Jesus, through his preaching from the pulpit, his teaching in the home, and by the example of how he lived his life.

Tim grew up mostly in Tennessee, Texas, and other southern states, where he spent his early years hunting, fishing, hiking, and exploring in the woods. After two frustrating years in college because he didn't know what he wanted to do with his life, he entered the workforce as an employee of a steel mill. Within ten years he had been through over thirty different jobs including welder, carpenter, crane operator, backhoe operator, concrete laborer, radio station manager, fast food store assistant manager, cash register salesman, forklift driver, dump truck driver, and factory worker. During that same period of time he had also tried twelve different home based business ideas and had looked at hundreds more.

By his early thirties success in any form had managed to totally elude him. His only claim to fame was that his ancestors on his mother's side were the Clanton's; some of whose descendants were involved in the shootout at the O.K. Coral in

Tombstone Arizona with Wyatt Earp and his hired gunmen.

As a result of finding a mentor he was able to turn his life around and develop a lifestyle that he could only have dreamed of in years past. Tim and his wife now own numerous corporations. Some of his time now is spent doing seminars and training sessions, and teaching others how to start a business of their own so that they too can develop a substantial residual income and have the option of getting out of the rat race. He also does presentations to churches, schools, civic organizations, and other groups about the need for more mentors in America, and about the lessons he learned from his mentor that made a major difference in his life.

As they were building their business Tim & his wife were featured in the May/June 1998 issue of 'Business Nashville' Magazine in an article entitled, 'Don't Stop to Shop', a reprint of which can be seen on Tim's Personal Page provided by Music City Publishing.

Go to: **www.musiccitypublishing.com**
and then to: 'Author Biographies and Personal Pages'
and then to: 'Business Nashville Magazine Reprint'.

In 2004 Tim Hendricks was inducted as a member into the 'International WHO'S WHO of Entrepreneurs'.

He also enjoys target shooting, fishing, golf, the outdoors, and traveling, which he does regularly with his wife of seventeen years, his two stepchildren, and five grandchildren. He currently resides in the city of Oak Hill, an exclusive area of Nashville, Tennessee.

Tim & Anna at the Atlantis Resort,
Paradise Island Bahamas

Parasailing 1,000 feet above Sarasta Bay, Florida.
Life is better with a mentor.

ORDER FORM

I would like to order _____ copies of *The Mentor*—The true story of an hourly factory employee who became financially independent.

For mail-in orders make checks payable and mailed to:

Music City Publishing
P.O. Box 41696
Nashville, Tn. 37204-1696

Your Name: _____

Address: _____

City:_____

State:_____ Zip:_____

email:_____

Signature:_____

Payment: Check ☐ Visa ☐ MasterCard ☐

Card Number: _____

Expiration Date:_____

Name on Card:_____

To order by Internet go to **www.musiccitypublishing.com**

Suggested Retail price $16.99
2-4 copies: 15.29 each (10% discount)
5-24 copies: 14.44 each (15% discount)
Free shipping on all orders in the Continental U.S.

For discounts on larger orders email:
discounts@musiccitypublishing.com